-ESSENTIAL-

MG

-ESSENTIAL-
MG

Graham Robson

MOTORBOOKS
INTERNATIONAL

DESIGNER: Philip Clucas MSIAD
COLOUR REPRODUCTION: Berkeley Square
Printed and Bound in China

This edition published in 2004 by Motorbooks
International, an imprint of MBI Publishing
Company, Galtier Plaza, Suite 200, 380 Jackson
Street, St. Paul, MN 55101-3885 USA

The information in this book is true and complete
to the best of our knowledge. All recommendations
are made without any guarantee on the part of the
author or Publisher, who also disclaim any liability
incurred in connection with the use of this data or
specific details.

We recognize that some words, model names and
designations, for example, mentioned herein are
the property of the trademark holder.
We use them for identification purposes only.
This is not an official publication.

Motorbooks International titles are also available at
discounts in bulk quantity for industrial or sales-
promotional use. For details write to Special Sales
Manager at Motorbooks International Wholesalers &
Distributors, Galtier Plaza, Suite 200, 380 Jackson
Street, St. Paul, MN 55101-3885 USA.

ISBN 0-7603-2003-9

Contents

Introduction

What is the world's most famous sports car? Ask any enthusiast that question and you will probably get a very predictable answer – MG. Now ask him what was the first sports car he ever owned? Or which he first drove? Or in which he took out his future partner? You'll usually get the same answer – MG. Famous in the 1930s, even more famous in the 1950s, and equally famous in the new century, MG is a great automotive survivor.

MGBs and MGFs .... sports cars, race cars, and record breaking cars old fashioned or super-modern...cheap or expensive. In eighty years MG has changed a lot. As with all famous brands, those running today's MG business would simply not recognize the way that original MGs were produced. And for that matter, surely, Cecil Kimber, who invented MG in 1923/1924, could never have expected to see such a modest operation to grow so large.

Eighty years ago, the very first MGs were built, in a corner of a garage in the middle of Oxford. Fifty years ago MG was already one of the most respected sports car makers in the world. Today, every MG is built at Longbridge, a marque vital to the survival of the MG Rover Group.

Modest Beginnings

William Morris started building cars at Cowley, near Oxford England, in 1913. To sell those cars, to service them, and to build

Below: *Cecil Kimber created the MG marque in 1924. Although this car is called 'Old Number One', it was actually a trials special, built in 1925.*

up product awareness, he founded Morris Garages, which had showrooms in Oxford itself. It was there, in 1922, that Cecil Kimber became general manager of that business.

Although Kimber was interested in motor sport, and in developing interesting new cars, his boss, William Morris, was not. In 1923, however, Kimber asked his workforce to produce a handful of re-bodied Morris Cowleys, which he originally called 'Chummy'. To follow them up, he also commissioned a few Raworth-bodied types. With rakish, open-top tourer body styles, these started a trend, which would soon become a sports car explosion.

Although Morris was happy to ignore sports cars, he was happy to make money out of these cars. Kimber, therefore, was given his head. Within a year he had evolved a modest range of re-bodied and re-engined Morris models, and invented the 'MG' badge – which was, of course, an acronym for 'Morris Garages'.

As the 1920s evolved, so did the MG motorcar. First of all there were 14/28 models, these being replaced in 1926 by the more powerful and restyled 14/40 types. In an age when sportscars tended to be expensive (like Bentley and Lagonda), or built in Europe, British enthusiasts took to the budget-priced MGs, and bought more of them. Nearly 200 cars were produced in 1925, and nearly 400 in 1927. Before long, therefore, the battle was not to sell cars, but to find somewhere to build them.

Early MGs were built at Albert Road, Oxford (it was owned by Morris Garages), but Kimber soon took over a corner of a Morris Motors radiator-building factory in Bainton Road, Oxford. That was in 1925, but by 1927 the walls were bursting yet again, and a small new factory was built in Edmund Road in Cowley, still very close to Oxford, and even closer to the Morris Motors assembly plant at Cowley.

By this time, the MG operation had turned from an indulgence to a growing business. Still personally owned, and financed, by William Morris, it was run by Kimber, who had abandoned the Morris garages job. Morris himself took little interest in 'his' sports car operation, though he was always anxious for it to turn an honest penny.

Late in the 1920s, Kimber decided that it was time to spread his, and MG's wings. First, he got approval to look at other Morris-owned businesses for his engines and running gear, and at the same time he was allowed to look for a much larger factory. In 1928 and 1929, therefore, he not only found a redundant factory building in Abingdon (a pleasant little town on the river Thames,

which was about seven miles south of Oxford itself), and he also forged links with Wolseley, so that they could supply him with overhead-camshaft engines, and their related transmissions. .

Abingdon

Only about 2,000 MGs had been built before the business moved to Abingdon, but the new premises, once run by the Pavlova Leather Company, were certainly large enough for any ambitions which Kimber might have, and it took only months to fit it out with simple assembly tracks, and make it suitable for motor car assembly.

Above: *MG moved to its legendary Abingdon factory in 1929. This was the original complex, which expanded considerably in later years.*

Not manufacture, you understand, for MG never made its own running gear, or its own bodies, but assembled the pieces. Over the years the modest little building at Abingdon would repeatedly be expanded. No matter who owned the MG trademark – and there would be several changes in the future – Abingdon would be the home of MG sports cars for the fifty years.

Above: *On sale from the end of 2003, the Ford-USA powered XPower SV was a mighty Supercar – very different from original MG types.*

Squaring their shoulders, and looking avidly ahead to an exciting – and diverse – future, in the early 1930s Kimber and MG then evolved a series of high-revving and rather specialized sports cars, and coupes. Some, like the little M-Type and J-Type Midgets, were true 'entry level' models, which captured the hearts of enthusiasts, and often made them MG slaves for life. Others, like the 18/80s, Magnas and Magnettes, were less overtly sporting, but slightly larger, and slightly more 'touring'.

MG also caught the motor racing bug at this time, developing more, and yet more, ambitious models. Factory-sponsored cars competed as far afield as the Mille Miglia in Italia, and by 1935 the latest 'works' machines were immensely fast, and successful.

Unhappily, the more than Kimber's MG spent on motorsport, the fewer MGs seemed to be sold. William Morris, knighted in 1928, and raised to the peerage, as Lord Nuffield in 1934, was unhappy about this, and set about the consolidation of his far-flung business empire. A new holding company, the Nuffield Organization, was set up in 1935, into which both Wolseley and MG were both swept.

MG now had to answer to a board of directors, not just Nuffield himself, and it was their hatchet man, Leonard Lord, who swept away all of MG's individual freedoms. From that moment, he decreed, MG's design office at Abingdon would close, new models would be designed at Cowley, and a series of Wolseley-based touring cars would be developed.

This, then, was the watershed. The last of the overhead-cam engined types, the PB Midgets and N-Type Magnettes, were soon swept away, to be replaced speedily by the T-Types, and the SVW range of touring MGs. It was a strategy that worked, for sales soared, and it was only the outbreak of war which brought real expansion to a halt.

After six years of war, MG was ready to get back into the private car business, which it did by producing TC Midgets, and the Y-Type sedan that had been designed in 1939. Exports rocketed – particularly to North America - sales rose, and would continue to rise, for this was the period when the world, not just the British, renewed its love of MG. The first cars with left-hand steering were built in the late 1940s, the first independent-front-suspension sports car (the TD) followed in 1950, and annual production breached 10,000 for the first time in 1952.

From that year, incidentally, Nuffield (and, therefore, MG) were swept into a new industry colossus, the British Motor Corporation (BMC), which meant that future MGs would be Austin, rather than Nuffield-based. Even so, the public liked what it saw, for the Y-Type Magnette saloons and the sweetly styled MGA sports cars were amazingly popular. Abingdon expanded, and became more versatile, especially after BMC moved Austin-Healey assembly into the building from 1957, and the small Austin-Healey Sprite/MG Midget family of sports cars were added soon afterwards.

Under BMC, the MG badge was then applied to various modified Austin sedans – this including the Magnette Mk III, and later the front-wheel-drive MG 1100/1300 – which were never assembled at Abingdon, but which increased the brand's sales enormously. At Abingdon the best-selling MGA was replaced by the monocoque MGB in 1962, a car that would eventually re-write all the records set by earlier MG sports cars.

The curse of British Leyland

BMC merged with Jaguar in 1966, then joined hands with Leyland in 1968, which meant that MG became one of many brands controlled by British Leyland. In the next decade plans for MG were made, plans were scrapped, mergers were suggested, then scrapped, and modified. In and around all this, the onset of new

North American safety and exhaust emission regulations cast a dark shadow over the future of the sports car business.

Because British Leyland was once inclined to merge MG with Triumph, bold new MG projects such as the EX234 and ADO21 projects were cancelled, and MGB derivatives like the MGC and the MGB GT V8 never prospered. British Leyland went bankrupt in 1975, the British government stepped in to keep the business afloat, and all interest in sports cars evaporated. The MGB and Midget models were both built throughout the 1970s, but had to die when they became obsolete. No successors were ever developed, and for a short time the MG disappeared completely. Worse- once the assembly lines at Abingdon were cleared, the bulldozers moved in, and the historic factory was flattened.

Then, in 1982 the re-birth of the marque began. BL (the latest name for British Leyland) introduced a series of front-wheel-drive MG badged sedans and hatchbacks – Metro, Maestro and Montego - all of which were upscale, faster, versions of Austin family cars. Through a period when BL became Austin-Rover, these sold surprisingly well. This was also the time when a bizarre mid-engined, four-wheel-drive version of the Metro was developed for rallying, but in spite of the MG badge it was an aberration.

Modern Times

After the British Government sold off the Austin-Rover business to British Aerospace in 1988, the new company was allowed to develop the RV-8, which resurrected the old MGB, with a V8 engine and a cosmetic makeover, but the more ambitious mid-engined MGF followed in 1995, just after BAe had sold out to BMW.

BMW tired of the loss-making Rover business, and threw it overboard (with a financial lifeboat) in 2000, but the new management took a deep breath and rejuvenated the MG brand yet again. New ZR, ZS and ZT types (including diesel engined versions) of conventional front-wheel-drive Rover types appeared in 1991, race and rally programs were added to bring pizzazz to the re-launch, and at the end of 2003 a new Supercar, the Xpower SV, went on sale.

This was the latest twist and turn in what had already been a fascinating 80-year history. There would be more surprises, for sure, in the years that followed.

1924-39 14/28 AND 14/40

Although the very first 'Morris Garages Specials' were the original two-seater Raworth-bodied 11.9hp models, it was the 14/28 Super Sports models of 1924 – 1926 that were the first series-production MGs. Inspired by Cecil Kimber, Morris Garages laid down a series of cars. These used highly modified versions of the existing Morris Cowley chassis, but were fitted with new and stylish bodies.

All used a version of the existing – and famous - 'bullnose' radiator style, but were the very first to carry the MG octagon badge which would become legendary as the years passed by.

'Bullnose', by the way, came from the profile of the radiator itself, and from the fact that the Morris radiator showed an ox in a ford (Morris cars were built near Oxford, so the inference was obvious).

Even by contemporary vintage standards, of course, there was little about these cars that made them unique – except for the styling, and the character that they all definitely had. Prices, however - £350 for an open-top two-seater, and £460 for a full four-door sedan – were lower than might have been expected, and demand was brisk.

This was the period in British motoring history when the 'bullnose' Morris was one of the fastest-selling cars on the British market – the other obvious contenders being the tiny Austin Seven, and the Ford Model T (which was made under license in a British Ford factory). Like its rivals, the 'bullnose' had a simple chassis, with channel side members, a flat head four-cylinder engine, a three-speed gearbox, and rod/cable-operated brakes. Half-elliptic leaf springs and friction-type dampers made up a totally conventional

Below: MG's original production car, the 14/28, was based on the contemporary Morris 'Bullnose' model, though with much smarter body styles.

specification. The 14/28 title was typical of British cars of its time – the '14' referring to the British system of taxing by notional horsepower rating, the '28' being close to the actual output itself.

Kimber and his colleagues then set out to improve on what they could use from the parent company. Although they could do little about the engine, and the transmission, they flattened the leaf springs (this lowered the chassis), altered the rake of the steering, and made the car feel sportier. Later there would be a different axle ratio, and optional wheel covers could make the cars look more streamlined, but it was the body styles themselves that made the cars so attractive.

Kimber himself was an accomplished, and committed, re-shaper of motorcars (it was sometimes said that he was always happy to find a new location to place an octagon motif!), and made sure that these 'Super Sports' looked good. Morris Garages (MG) never made their own coachwork, however, for much of the coachwork was contracted out to Carbodies of Coventry.

Already there was a choice of two-seater or four-seater Roadsters, a sedan, and even a Landaulette: the majority of cars sold had Roadster coachwork, and therefore were the first true MG sports cars. For the next four years these pioneering MGs followed the changes made to the Cowley and Oxford models that were the design parents. Accordingly, when the Morris cars' wheelbase increased by six inches, so did that of the 14/28, and after two years, when the Morris style was changed to a new flat-nose radiator, so was that of the MG.

It was, however, the overall style that appealed so much. Two-tone color schemes were introduced (some of them featured unpainted aluminum panels), and there was a popular list of options, so it was not long before the tiny workshops at Alfred Lane, in Oxford, were overcrowded. A move soon had to be made to Bainton Road (in a corner of the Morris factory which built radiators) – but this was only the first of several such shifts in the 1920s.

The change from 'bullnose' to 'flat radiator' style came late in 1926, and was accompanied by a completely new chassis frame – wider, shorter in the wheelbase, and altogether heavier than before. This immediately took the edge off the 14/28's already limited performance – a 60mph top speed was possible, quite brisk for the period, but it looks slow these days, though sales held up remarkably well.

At the same time, the technicians worked through the chassis, providing Marles instead of Morris steering, Hartford instead of Smith dampers, a new small brake servo, and a re-worked cable-braking layout. Open-hub wire-spoke wheels were adopted, along with the latest type of softer-riding 'balloon' tires.

MILESTONE FACTS

- These were the very first cars to carry the MG octagon badge that would become legendary as the years passed by.

- The 14/28 title was typical of British cars of its time – the '14' referring to the British system of taxing by notional horsepower rating, the '28' being close to the actual output itself.

- Morris Garages (MG) never made their own coachwork- much of the coachwork was contracted out to Carbodies of Coventry.

- Two-tone color schemes were introduced (some of them featured unpainted aluminum panels), and there was a popular list of options.

- The change from 'bullnose' to 'flat radiator' style came late in 1926, and was accompanied by a completely new chassis frame – wider, shorter in the wheelbase, and altogether heavier than before.

- The flat-radiator cars eventually became known as 14/40s, though the engine's actual power output was certainly no more than 35bhp.

- As before, only right-hand steering was available, for Morris/MG was really only interested in selling to British and 'Empire' markets: the first left-hand-drive MGs would not be built until the late 1940s.

Incidentally, although there does not seem to have been any rigid changeover point, the engine was slightly up-rated at the same time (MG found time, and space, to partly strip out the engines, fettle them, and put them together again). The flat-radiator cars eventually became known as 14/40s, though the engine's actual power output was certainly no more than 35bhp.

Because Morris prices were so ruthlessly controlled, MG prices actually came down too – with the two-seater Roadster now selling for £340. As before, only right-hand steering was available, for Morris/MG was really only interested in selling to British and 'Empire' markets: the first left-hand-drive MGs would not be built until the late 1940s.

Within a year assembly had to move again, this time to a new building in Edmund Road, Oxford, and it was there that the 14/40 reached its maturity, with more then ten cars being produced in a good week. Soon, however, demand for the Cowley/Oxford-based machine began to ebb away (it was no longer a novel design, and rivals had begun to appear), and the last cars of all were produced early in 1929. By that time, in any case, MG's prospects had been transformed, by the arrival of the tiny new M-Type Midget.

(Left) The dickey seat of the 14/40.

(Left, Below) The 14/40's dashboard was simply equipped.

(Left) Engine turned detailing on a 14/40-bonnet-panel, a nice 1920s touch.

(Below) Horns were loud and clear on 1920s-style British sports cars.

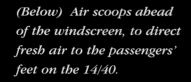

(Below) Air scoops ahead of the windscreen, to direct fresh air to the passengers' feet on the 14/40.

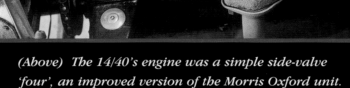

(Above) The 14/40's engine was a simple side-valve 'four', an improved version of the Morris Oxford unit.

SPECIFICATIONS

Production: 398/829

Body styles: Sedan and open sports

Construction: Steel chassis, wood/steel or wood/aluminum bodies

Engine: Four-cylinder, 1,802cc.

Power Output: 35bhp

Transmission: Three-speed manual

Suspension: Front – beam, leaf springs, rear - beam axle, leaf springs

Brakes: Front drums, rear drum

Maximum speed: 60 mph (96 km/h)

0-50mph (0-80 km/h): 25sec

Fascinating badge detail on the 14/40 - on this car the MG octagon was inside the 'Morris Oxford' lettering.

1928-33 *18/80 Six*

MG's second series-production car, the 18/80, was also based on a current Morris design – that of the much larger, heavier and more costly Morris Six. For the first time, this was an MG with a six-cylinder engine. Compared with the old 14/40 range, which was soon to disappear from the range, this car was more costly - £485 for the open Tourer, and £555 for the four-door sedan.

Although the general layout was similar to that of the 14/40, no components were shared. The sturdy new chassis frame ran on a 114in/2,896mm wheelbase, with 48in./1,219mm wheel tracks, while the engine was a massive new six-cylinder unit of 2,468cc, with a single overhead camshaft type of cylinder head and valve gear. A three-speed gearbox was standard, and the brakes were operated using rods and cables.

For this new model MG's owner, Sir William Morris allowed Kimber's team to design a completely new chassis frame, which they lowered as much as possible, building in as many sports car features as their budget would allow. Kimber had much to do with the general style and layout of the bodies. As with the 14/40, these were manufactured by Carbodies, in Coventry.

This, by the way, was the very first MG to be fitted with a noble new radiator style, one that had a mesh grille, and the octagon badge at its peak. That style set a standard for the next twenty-five years, for it would not be until 1953 that a new

Below: MG assembly at Abingdon in 1930, with 18/80s closest to the camera., and a line-up of M-Type Midgets behind.

model (the TF) incorporated any style that was at all different.

By this time, MG had great ambitions. Having designed a new frame, they were also allowed to make changes to the engine. For their special needs, it had a stronger cylinder block, twin SU carburetors, and a power output of 60bhp. In every way this was a faster, more sturdy, and more purposeful car than the 14/40, though it was aimed at a rather different market. Even so, MG hoped that the new 18/80 would sell at least as briskly as the 14/40 had ever done, particularly as early magazine road tests showed that it could reach 80mph.

In the meantime, the arrival of a further, tiny, MG (the M-Type Midget) meant that the business was once again running out of space. Although a few 18/80s were assembled in Oxford, most of them would be built at the Abingdon factory, which served MG so well until the MGB was killed off in 1980. As before, there was a choice of body styles, which included two-seater or four-seater Tourers, and smart though rather angular four-seater sedans.

Only one year after the original 18/80 had been launched. MG announced a further-developed version, the 18/80 Mk II, which would run alongside the Mark I for the next two seasons. Compared with the original, the revised version was more purposeful, and more thoughtfully equipped. The chassis frame itself had been beefed up, the wheel tracks were increased to 52in./1,321mm, and the axles, springs, dampers and steering were all fleshed out to match. The drum brakes were increased in size – from 12in./305mm to 14in./356mm – and, most important of all, there was now a four-speed gearbox.

The good news was that this was a very capable car, and a real improvement, but the bad news that it was at least 300lb/136kg heavier than before, which meant that the performance and acceleration had actually been degraded. Prices started at £625, and since this was the moment at which the British market began to slip back into recession, sales were hard to find.

Even so, by the end of 1929, MG was making three times as many cars as it had made in 1928 (the M-Type Midget was responsible for much of this boost), and for the two types of 18/80 there was a choice of twelve body styles, though some Mk IIs were merely widened versions of earlier Mk I types.

Although only 236 Mk IIs would be sold in a four year period (which means that this model could surely not have been profitable), the 18/80 was important as the first MG sports car where all the chassis had been specially designed for its purpose, and where the classic (later legendary) radiator style was established.

MILESTONE FACTS

- MG's second series-production car, the 18/80, was also based on a current Morris design – that of the much larger, heavier and more costly Morris Six.

- For the first time, this was an MG with a six-cylinder engine.

- For this new model MG's owner, Sir William Morris allowed Kimber's team to design a completely new chassis frame, that they lowered as much as possible building in as many sports car features as their budget would allow.

- This was the very first MG to be fitted with a noble new radiator style, one that had a mesh grille, and the octagon badge at its peak. That style set a standard for the next twenty-five years.

- Only one year after the original 18/80 had been launched. MG announced a further-developed version, the 18/80 Mk II, which would run alongside the Mark I for the next two seasons. The good news was that this was a real improvement, but the bad news that it was at least 300lb/136kg heavier than before, which meant that the performance and acceleration had actually been degraded.

- For the ever-ambitious Kimber, this was also his chance to build MG's first racing sports car. In 1930 his team developed the 18/80 Mk III, which was a four-seater sports car designed purely for motorsport.

- This, therefore, was the point at which MG cast off its early connections with Morris cars in favor of building totally specialized models.

Not only that, but for the ever-ambitious Kimber, this was also his chance to build MG's first racing sports car. In 1930 his team developed the 18/80 Mk III, which was a four-seater sports car designed purely for motorsport. The engine was boosted, first to 83bhp, and finally to a rather perilous 96bhp, and because the lightweight body was as small and flimsy as international regulations would apply, this was a car which would handsomely exceed 90mph.

However, because it was priced at £895, it only had a limited appeal, and only five such cars were ever produced. Survivors, naturally, are highly prized today.

18/80 Mk I assembly ended in mid-1931, but the Mk II remained on sale until mid-1933. By this time the Abingdon factory was full up, flooded by the much smaller Midgets, Magnas and Magnettes. This, therefore, was the point at which MG cast off its early connections with Morris cars in favor of building totally specialized models.

SPECIFICATIONS

Production: 740

Body styles: Sedan and open sports

Construction: Steel chassis, wood and steel bodies

Engine: Six-cylinders, 2,468cc.

Power Output: 60bhp

Transmission: Three-speed manual/(Mk II) four-speed manual

Suspension: Front – beam, leaf springs, rear - beam axle, leaf springs

Brakes: Front drums, rear drum

Maximum speed: 80 mph (129 km/h)

0-50mph (0-80km/h): 16sec

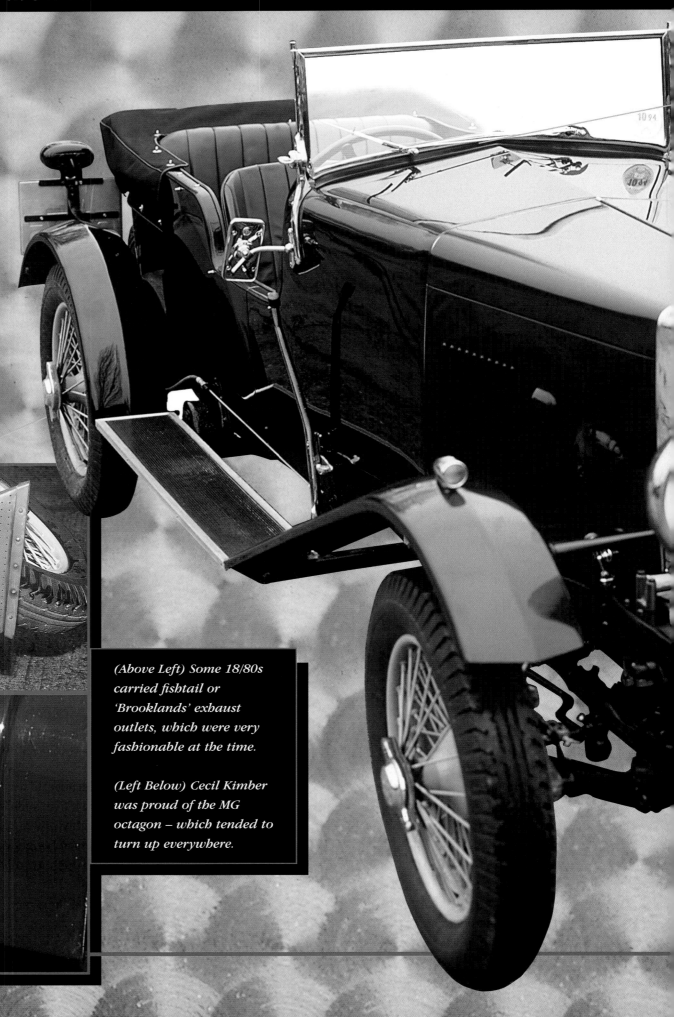

(Above Left) Some 18/80s carried fishtail or 'Brooklands' exhaust outlets, which were very fashionable at the time.

(Left Below) Cecil Kimber was proud of the MG octagon – which tended to turn up everywhere.

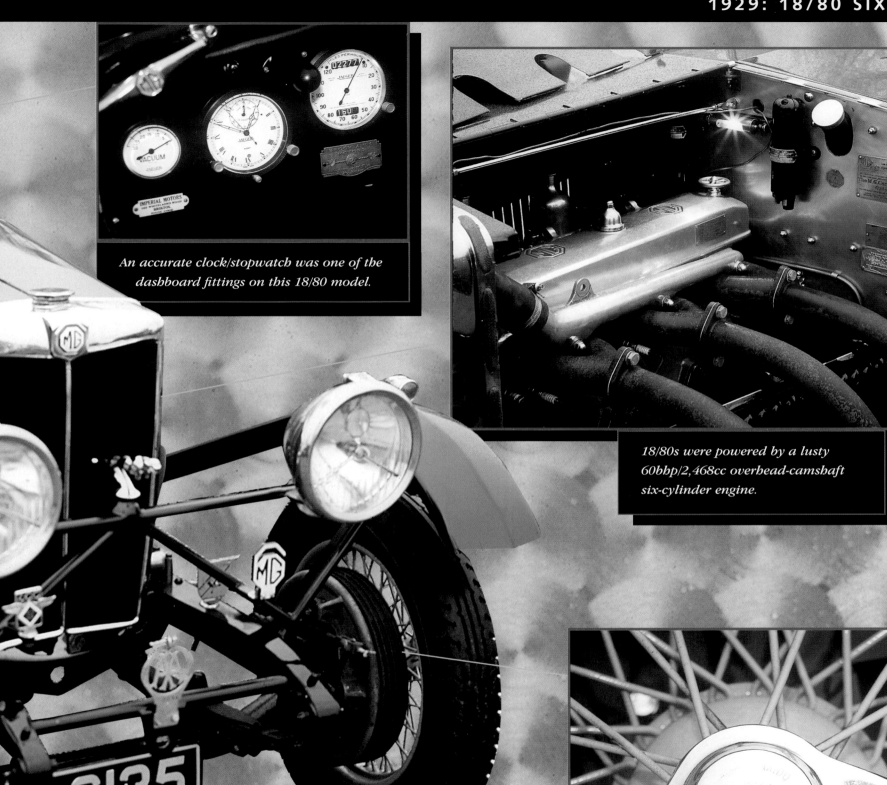

An accurate clock/stopwatch was one of the dashboard fittings on this 18/80 model.

18/80s were powered by a lusty 60bhp/2,468cc overhead-camshaft six-cylinder engine.

(Right) Centre-lock wire wheels – an essential fitting on all such British sports cars for many years.

1928-32 *M-Type Midget*

In October 1928, MG changed the face of sports car motoring – for ever. Tucked away on the MG stand at the Olympia Motor Show was the very first prototype of a tiny little two-seater which would establish a new MG pedigree – the 847cc-engined M-Type Midget.

Although it was cheap and cheerful – it would only reach 64mph, but then it only cost £175 – it brought sports car motoring within reach of the middle classes, instead of the idle rich. It was the very first of a whole series of 'Midgets', which would not finally die out for half-a-century.

In developing the M-Type, MG achieved their goal by building what was really little more than a re-bodied Morris Minor chassis. This tiny machine – it had only a 78in/1,981mm wheelbase and 42in/1,067mm wheel tracks – was graced by a brand-new four-cylinder engine that Wolseley (another company owned by Sir William Morris) had designed. This featured single overhead camshaft valve gear and, incidentally, a vertically mounted dynamo at the front of the power unit, whose armature shaft also drove the camshaft itself.

Although the entire car was build severely down to a price – features like bolt-on wire spoke wheels, and a three-speed gearbox spelt that out – the two-seater body was pleasant, and attractive. Carbodies were paid a mere £6.50 for each complete, painted, shell, which was a pragmatic combination of wood, canvas and some steel paneling, complete with what was now the characteristic MG radiator grille.

Because it was so light (1,120lb/508kg, unladen) even with only 20bhp the performance was brisk by the standards of the day. After MG had got together with Wolseley to push that peak up to 27bhp, at the time no one ever called the M-Type slow.

The M-Type arrived at exactly the right time – in 19328/1929 the British car market was buoyant, and even when it turned down in 1930 it was the cheapest cars that soldiered on with the least trauma. Demand for the new Midget was stronger than for any previous MG, so it must have been a relief to MG that deliveries could begin from Edmund Road in March 1929, and that the complete assembly lines were moved to the newly purchased Abingdon factory later in that year. By that time, Midget production was more than equal to all other MG models being built at the new factory.

The Midget's performance, if not its creature comforts, compared well with the existing 14/40, though this car was due to be dropped within the year. Not only did it accelerate as well, but it also cost only half as much. No wonder, then, that Britain's weekly motoring magazine, The Autocar, suggested that: The MG Midget will make sports car history.'

Evolution of this original 847cc-engined MG was rapid. The first race-prepared Midgets raced at Brooklands in 1929, and it was a result of sturdy endurance performances that at the 1930 London Motor Show the engine was boosted from 20bhp to 27bhp (by using the racecars' camshaft timing). Privately owned cars began to appear in races and rallies, all round the world, so in 1931 Kimber inspired the building a very effective little racecar version, the C-Type.

Below: *The C-Type Montlhery was a racing derivative of the M-Type Midget, always very successful in its capacity class.*

Above: *The original M-Type Midget, launched in 1928, was based on the new Morris Minor chassis, and had a light and simple two-seater body.*

MILESTONE FACTS

- This was the very first of a whole series of 'Midgets', which would not finally die out for half-a-century.

- It featured a single overhead camshaft engine with a vertically mounted dynamo at the front of the power unit, whose armature shaft also drove the camshaft itself.

- MG deliveries began from Edmund Road in March 1929, and the complete assembly lines were moved to the newly-purchased Abingdon factory later in that year*

- This machine, soon labeled 'Montlhery' after successful speed runs at the French track, had a much lowered chassis frame, a short-stroke 746cc supercharged version of the high-revving little engine, a four-speed gearbox and with a smoothed out front cowl to the body it would reach up to 100mph. *

- Between 1928 and 1932, though, the original M-Type was the mainstay of MG's business, for no fewer than 3,235 would be produced – often at the rate of up to 30 cars every week. .
  *Those were the days, when British cars had no heaters, and when the wind howled in around the edges of soft tops and side curtains.

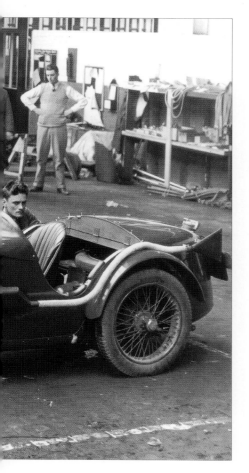

This machine, soon labeled 'Montlhery' after successful speed runs at the French track, had a much lowered chassis frame, a short-stroke 746cc supercharged version of the high-revving little engine, a four-speed gearbox and with a smoothed out front cowl to the body it would reach up to 100mph. No fewer than 14 cars were produced in time for the 1931 Brooklands Double Twelve (hours, that is) race, where they won the race outright, benefiting from a generous handicap that would be slashed to ribbons for future races.

As a spin-off model, MG then produced the D-Type Midget of 1931-1932, which used a longer-wheelbase version of the Montlhery's new chassis frame, but retained the simple running gear of the M-Type Midget in a four-seater open or closed top body style. It was this sort of mix-and-match product planning which allowed MG to make every possible sale in the early 1930s.

Between 1928 and 1932, though, the original M-Type was the mainstay of MG's business, for no fewer than 3,235 would be produced – often at the rate of up to 30 cars every week. Almost all of them would sport the same open-top two-seater style, complete with a sharply pointed' boat-tail' rear end, but in addition there was a closed version of this chassis that rather destroyed the lines, but made it a more habitable car in winter conditions.

M-Types, you see, were very small, with a very narrow cockpit, and if two occupants were not close friends at the start of a long journey, they either became so, or vowed never to speak to each other again, by its end. Passengers' legs were placed to each side of the transmission, and were very close to the engine itself, which did at least provide some heat when the running gear was warmed up. Those were the days, of course, when British cars had no heaters, and when the wind howled in around the edges of soft tops and side curtains.

By 1932, however, it was time for a new model to take over. Improving on the appeal of the M-Type Midget would not be easy, but the J1/J2 cars that took over would do just that.

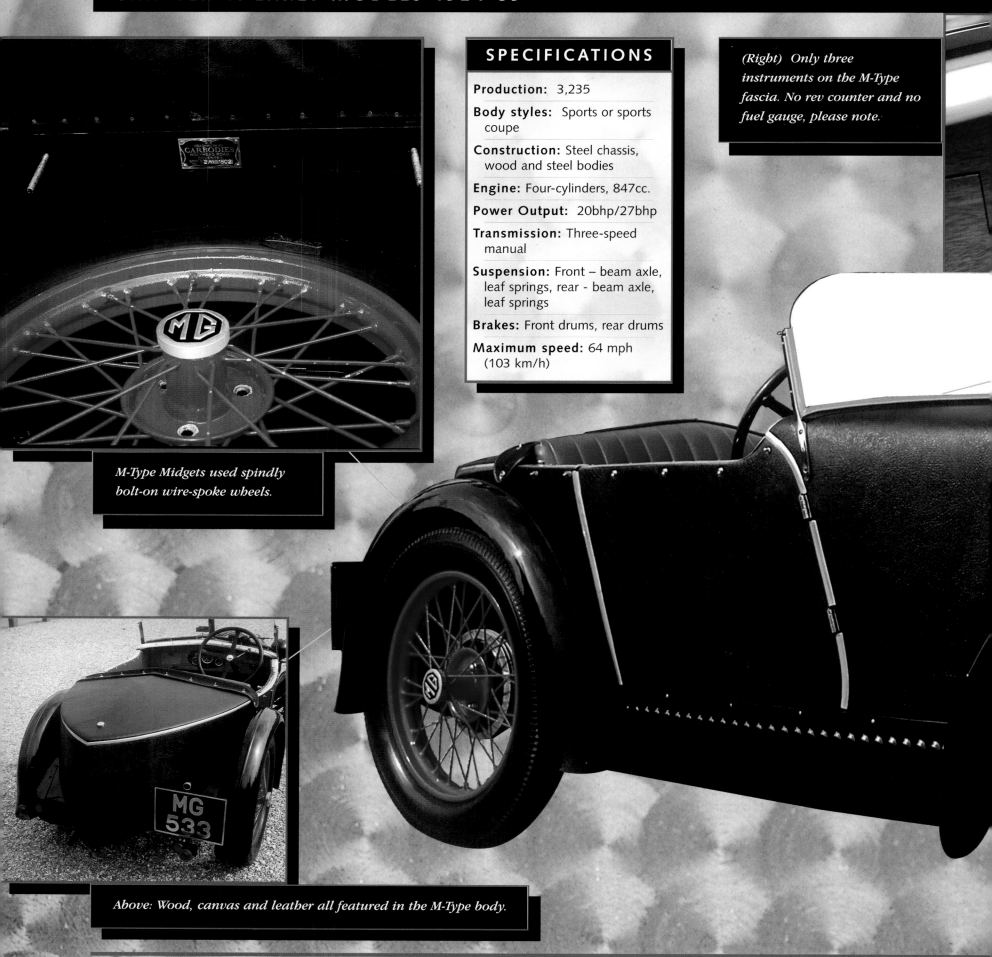

SPECIFICATIONS

Production: 3,235

Body styles: Sports or sports coupe

Construction: Steel chassis, wood and steel bodies

Engine: Four-cylinders, 847cc.

Power Output: 20bhp/27bhp

Transmission: Three-speed manual

Suspension: Front – beam axle, leaf springs, rear - beam axle, leaf springs

Brakes: Front drums, rear drums

Maximum speed: 64 mph (103 km/h)

(Right) Only three instruments on the M-Type fascia. No rev counter and no fuel gauge, please note.

M-Type Midgets used spindly bolt-on wire-spoke wheels.

Above: Wood, canvas and leather all featured in the M-Type body.

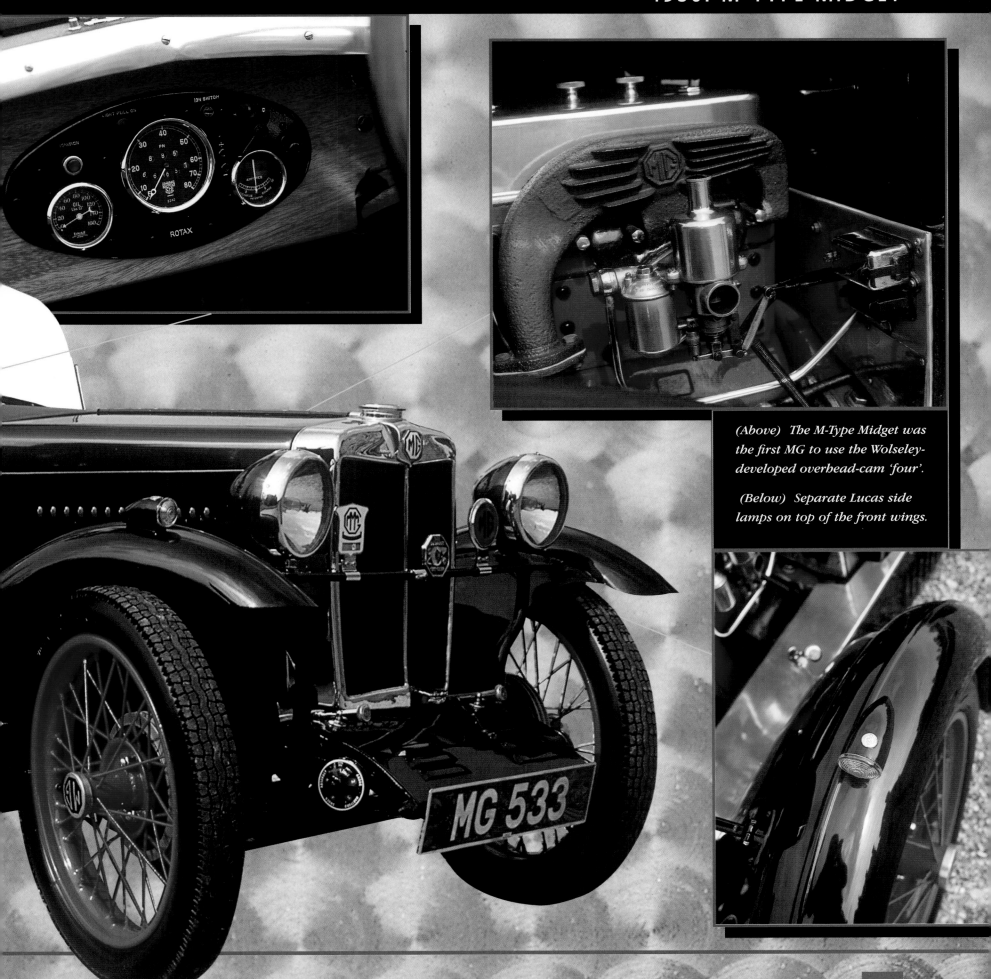

(Above) The M-Type Midget was the first MG to use the Wolseley-developed overhead-cam 'four'.

(Below) Separate Lucas side lamps on top of the front wings.

MG 533

1931-32 *F-Type Magna*

Even though car sales were hit badly by the recession in the early 1930s, MG pressed ahead with new models at Abingdon. Cecil Kimber realised that he needed a new six-cylinder car to replace the ageing 18/80 model, which led to the launch of the F-Type Magna in 1931.

This was the first of a series of overhead-cam six-cylinder engined cars – Magnas and Magnettes – which would head the MG product line in the next five years.

Because there was neither the time, the money, nor the facilities for MG to evolve yet another all-new car, the Magna had to be based, closely, on what MG already had, and what it knew. Accordingly, although it was originally launched as the 12/70 (which meant that MG was claiming 70 developed horsepower for the 1.3-liter engine), in fact the Magna produced less than 40bhp, and had a top speed of only 73mph.

In effect, here was another neat little sports car, in the 'Abingdon-style', which combined a lengthened version of the C-Type Montlhery chassis frame, complete with the same narrow wheel tracks, the same axles and brakes, but this time with a six-cylinder engine, a four-speed transmission, and enough space to provide more practical seating for four willing passengers.

In many ways the Magna engine was a six-cylinder version of the M-Type Midget's 'four'. As before, it had been designed, developed, and was manufactured by Wolseley, sharing much of the machine tooling already in place. Although it was closely based on the Wolseley Hornet power unit, MG tried to disguise this by adding cosmetic sheet metal panels to disguise its origins, though few customers were fooled. And why keep to an overhead-camshaft power unit, which was costly to manufacture? The reason, in part, was that MG's big rivals, Singer, also sold sports cars with such an advanced layout, and MG did not want to be out-gunned.

Because it was longer, heavier and significantly faster, the Magna sold to a rather different clientele. At a time when M-Type Midgets were priced at £165 (or £185 with a steel paneled body), F-Type Magna prices ranged from £250 for the open-top car to £289 for the closed type. The new car was smoother, more refined, and had a considerably better-equipped interior than the M-Type Midget, but even though it ran on a 94in./2,388mm wheelbase it still had an extremely small (some called it snug) cabin.

MG, however, had struck the right note with this car, which was launched at a time when MG and the British motoring market both sought a boost. Customers hit by the depression decided to trade down from their larger cars, and found an F-Type Magna seductive, while those who felt brave enough to trade-up from the tiny Midgets also found the Magna very suitable for their needs.

In less than two years, no fewer than 1,250 such cars were produced, in a whole variety of two-seater, four-seater, open sports and closed styled, including what was called a 'Salonette'. All of them naturally shared the same front-end style, and that by-now familiar radiator grille.

For MG, however, who might now be described as a hyper active organization, it was asking too much for them to leave this design alone. After the first season, not only did the company offer it with 12in. (instead of puny 8in.) drum brakes, but the type numbers also became f2 (two-seaters) and f3 (four-seater types).

These, by any current standards, were cars that became fashionable. Whereas the little M-

Right: *The Magna spare wheel was fixed to the very tail of the body shell.*

Type Midgets had been sweet, but tiny, built down to a price, and not very fast, here was a rakish MG which was longer, looked more upscale (a car for swells, as it was sometimes described), and seemed ideal as the kind of sports car with which to swish up to the country club, the tennis court, or the country house weekend.

MILESTONE FACTS

- This was the first of a series of overhead-cam six-cylinder engined cars – Magnas and Magnettes – which would head the MG product line in the next five years.

- Although it was closely based on the Wolseley Hornet power unit, MG tried to disguise this by adding cosmetic sheet metal panels to disguise its origins, though few customers were fooled. *Customers hit by the depression decided to trade down from their larger cars, and found an F-Type Magna seductive as here was a rakish MG which was longer, looked more upscale (a car for swells, as it was sometimes described), and seemed ideal as the sort of sports car with which to swish up to the country club, the tennis court, or the country house weekend.

- Wheel tracks were widened, and the engines were mildly improved by the use of a new cross-flow cylinder head, but the biggest advance of all was that a new-type pre-selector transmission became standard.

By this time Cecil Kimber had worked out, very accurately, what his clientele wanted – not the highest performance, but the most endearing character, and not the highest possible specification, but the best and most obvious value for money.

No one, however, ever described the Magna as a fast car, and if only MG could have been given their chance on this car, they could certainly have increased the performance of the smooth six-cylinder power. This was, however, the right car, at the right price, and Kimber left it at that.

Towards the end of the F-Type's run, however, MG evolved yet another type of six-cylinder car, the K-Type Magnette, which was loosely based on F-Type running gear, but was much more specialized and more expensive. The chassis was the same as before (and a long-wheelbase type was also available), the wheel tracks were widened, and the engines were mildly improved by the use of a new cross-flow cylinder head, but the biggest advance of all was that a new-type pre-selector transmission became standard.

All this came at a cost – the average K-Type Magnette was priced at £100 more than a Magna – and this reduced demand, so that a mere 171 K1 and K2 types would be sold in the next two years. Their legacy, however, was that they donated their DNA to two further pedigrees of six-cylinder MG, the racing-type K3 Magnette, and the L-Type Magna, both of which would go on sale in 1933.

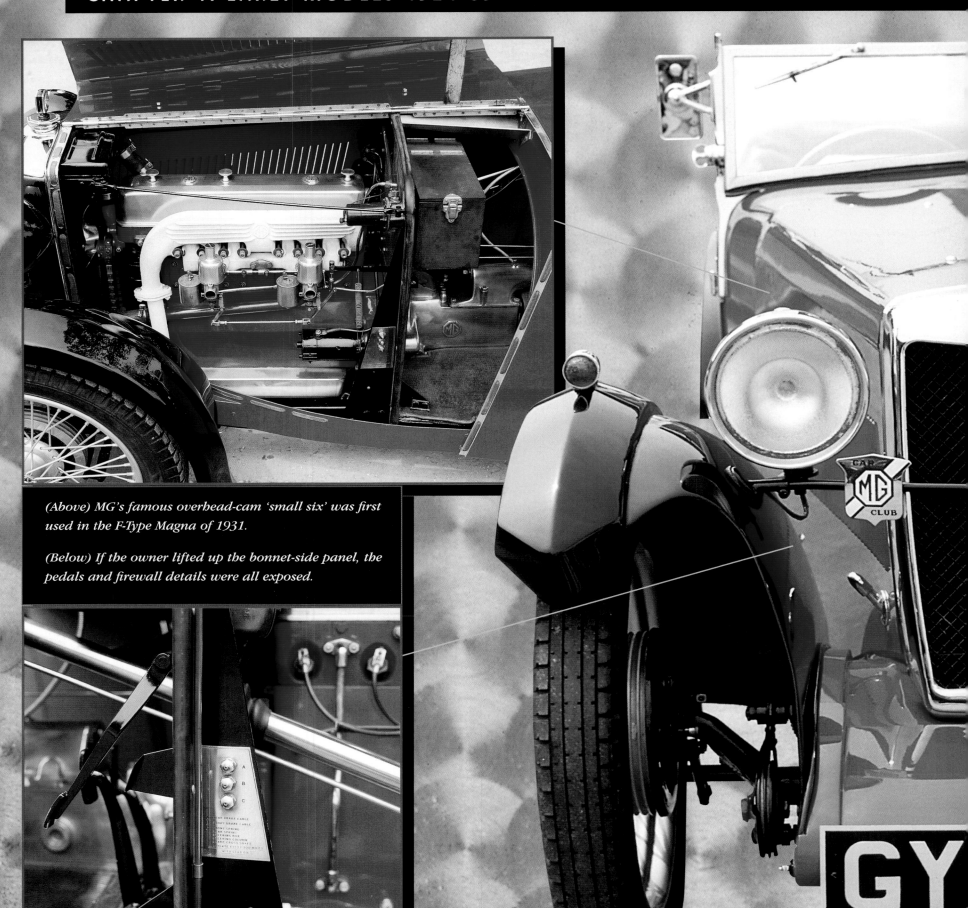

(Above) MG's famous overhead-cam 'small six' was first used in the F-Type Magna of 1931.

(Below) If the owner lifted up the bonnet-side panel, the pedals and firewall details were all exposed.

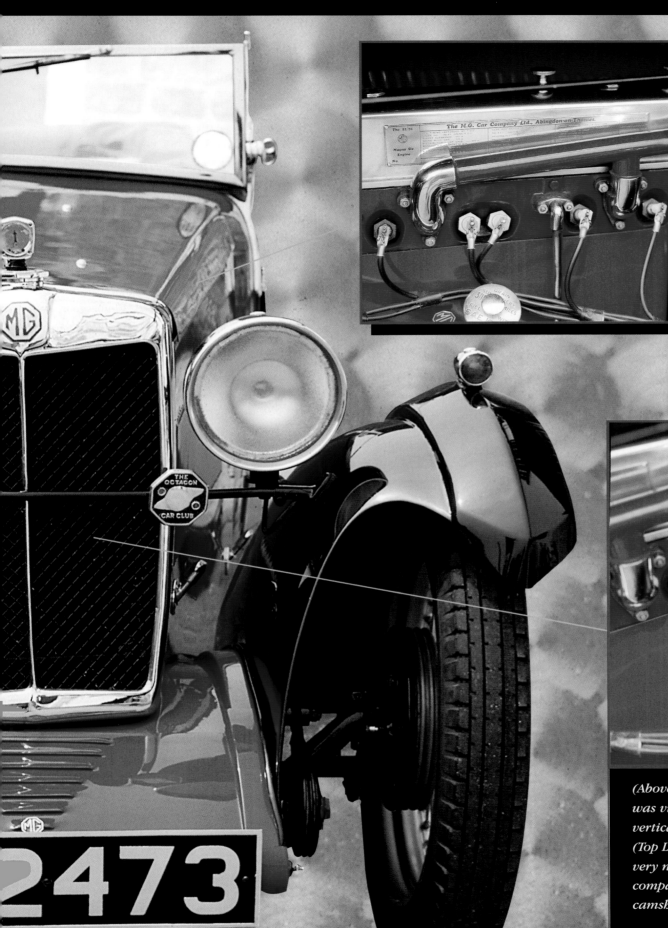

SPECIFICATIONS

Production: 1,250

Body styles: Two-seat and fou8r-seat, open and closed

Construction: Steel chassis, wood and steel bodies

Engine: Six-cylinders, 1,271cc.

Power Output: 37bhp

Transmission: Four-speed manual

Suspension: Front – beam axle, leaf springs, rear - beam axle, leaf springs

Brakes: Front drums, rear drums

Maximum speed: 75 mph (121 km/h)

(Above) Drive to the overhead camshaft was via the rotating armature of the vertically mounted generator.
(Top Left) The six-cylinder engine was very neatly detailed, and the MG company advertised its product on the camshaft cover.

1932-34 *J1* AND *J2 Midget*

Ever since MG introduced the J-Type Midget in 1932, enthusiasts have gone starry-eyed over its qualities. As a direct replacement for the original Midget the M-Type, here was a new sports car which was faster, prettier, more practical, and an all-round improvement. It was exactly the right car that MG needed to get them through the trade depression, and to build a platform for future, even faster, even more sporting little MG s.

Without spending a fortune on research, or re-tooling, MG had produced a car that instantly made the very basic M-Type look old fashioned. Most importantly, they had found ways of extracting more power from the little 847cc engine, and the styling was a real advance, even though prices had risen only slightly, to £199.50. J1 and J2 types (the title depended on the body styles chosen) would be firm favorites for the next two years.

Although quite a number of major components were carried over from previous models, there was real innovation too. The J-Type was the first MG to use a chassis frame with a 86in./2,184mm wheelbase, though it was a direct development of D-Type and Montlhery Midget designs. The axles, with their slim 42in./1,067mmtread dimensions, were the same as ever, as were the rather inadequate eight-inch diameter cable-operated drum brakes. Even the four-speed gearbox

was an evolution of that already found on other Midgets and Magnas.

The major innovations were in the engine, and in the body style. Although the engine was still the familiar, high-revving, overhead-cam 847cc 'four', its peak power had been pushed up to 36bhp, which was almost on a par with the output of the much larger six cylinder Magnas and Magnettes. For it came complete with a cross-flow cylinder head and twin SU carburetors.

The body style, an obvious advance on that of the C-Type Montlhery and the larger Magna, featured a double-humped

Below: *Once MG settled on this swept wing body style, they had created the classic style of the 1930s. Enthusiasts loved it.*

scuttle/cowl profile, and cutaway doors. These cutaways brought two benefits – one was that the driver could find a bit more elbow room when sawing away at the steering wheel, the other being that it allowed two occupants to find a little bit more space inside what was still rather a cramped cockpit.

As with previous Midgets, the J-type was also made available in two-seater sports (the J2), and in four-seater open and closed types (J1). According to MG's own managers, no stylist had been allowed anywhere near this car at the prototype stage. MG staff already knew what they wanted, they thought they knew what the customers would enjoy, and they also knew what their coachwork suppliers (Carbodies, notably) could supply. The J2, in particular, was such a pretty little car that all these assumptions were fulfilled – yet within a year the style had also been given long, sweeping, front wings, which made it appear even sleeker and more purposeful than ever.

Customers, for sure, were always ready to wring the last ounce, and the last mile, out of their J2's performance. Although this was a credit to MG, it also brought the company some embarrassment. The first J2 released to the press for performance testing – The Autocar, no less – was fitted with a more powerful, non-standard engine. Although MG was delighted to see this car credited with a top speed of 80.35mph, no private-owner's car could match that figure, and there was a flood of complaint about a lack of performance. The 847cc engine, in any case, still ran on a two-bearing crankshaft, and if over-revved there were several instances of these breaking in two, with catastrophic results.

As ever, MG then used the new J2 to mix-and-match chassis components and elements of the new body style on new models. Almost immediately the basic body shell, although modified for a longer wheelbase, was made available on the six-cylinder Magna chassis, but it was the J3 and J4 Midgets of 1933 that made more of an impact. Once again, MG was looking for motor racing

success, so these cars were effectively built as replacements for the earlier Montlhery Midgets, though with the J2's longer wheelbase frame and (in the case of the J4 much larger and more effective brakes, these actually being 'borrowed' from the F-Type Magna. J3s (of which only 22 cars would be built) and J4s (just nine) were all fitted with the very latest supercharged version of the 746cc engine, and were aimed squarely at the 750cc capacity class limit.

When fitted with the most powerful 'sprint' engines – MG never boasted of figures, but these must have approached 60bhp – the slim, light-bodied J4s were almost 'too fast for chassis', which may explain why the next generation of MG racing sports cars would be built around the six-cylinder chassis. J4s, even so, offered good publicity for MG, for their style looked almost exactly like that of the J2 road car. It was only when one looked closely that one could see the body bulge, up front, which hid the supercharger, and the fact that there were no doors cut in to the body sides.

All in all, the J1 and J2 models restored MG's fortunes immediately after the worst of the Depression. And they laid the foundations for the next important small MG – the P-Type that would take over in 1934.

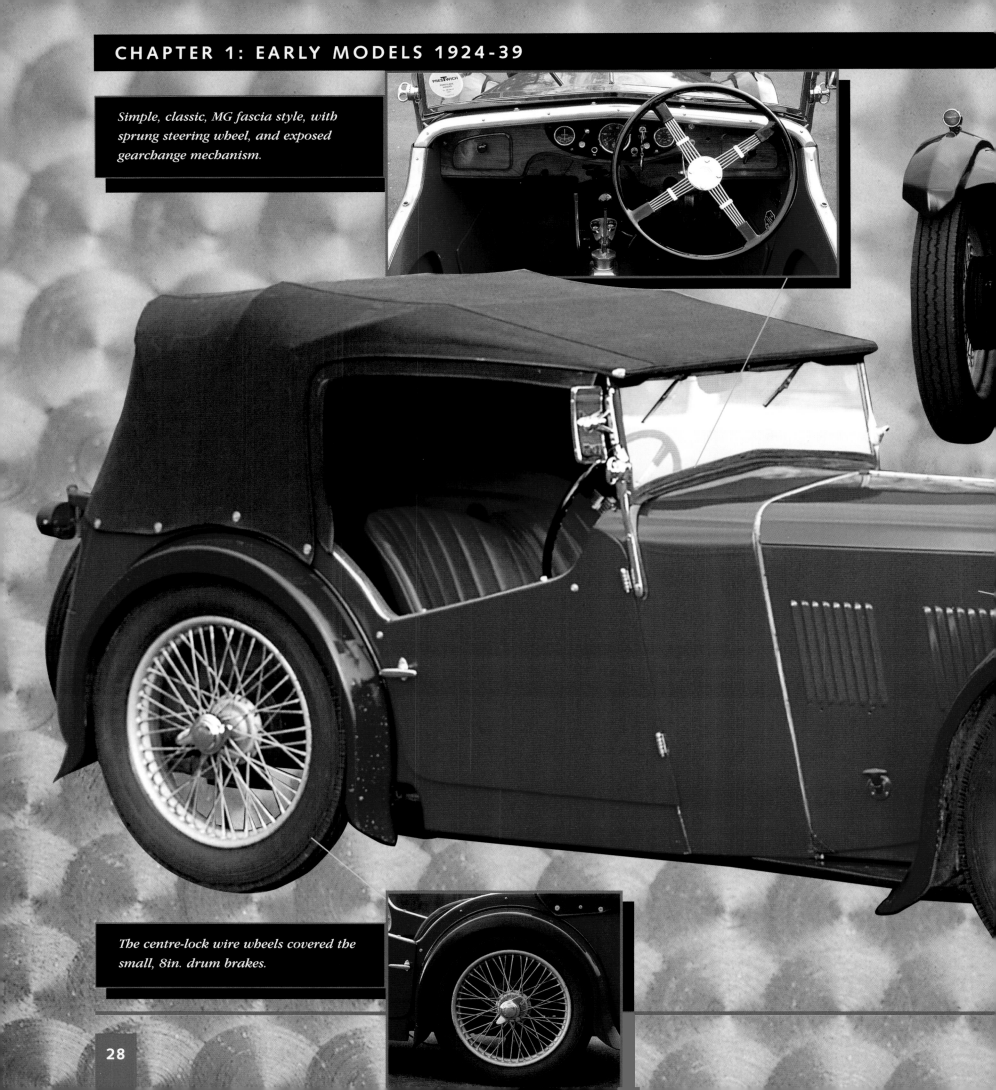

Simple, classic, MG fascia style, with sprung steering wheel, and exposed gearchange mechanism.

The centre-lock wire wheels covered the small, 8in. drum brakes.

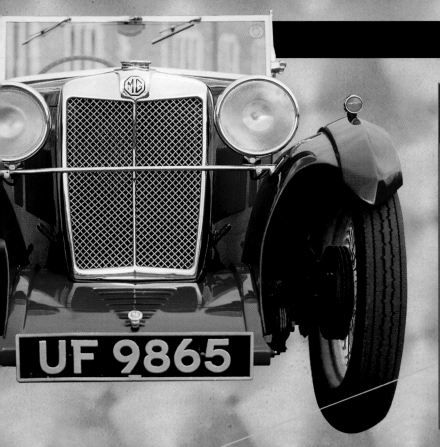

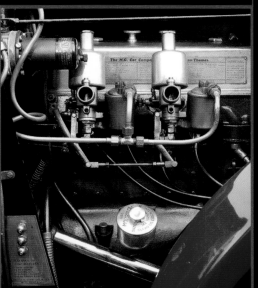

Twin SU carburetors on the cross-flow 847cc engine.

SPECIFICATIONS

Production: 380(J1)/2,083(J2)

Body styles: Two-seat (J2) and four-seat, open or closed (J1)

Construction: Steel chassis, wood and steel bodies

Engine: Four-cylinders, 847cc.

Power Output: 36bhp

Transmission: Four-speed manual

Suspension: Front – beam axle, leaf springs, rear - beam axle, leaf springs

Brakes: Front drums, rear drums

Maximum speed: 75mph (121 km/h)

Naturally an octagon was cast in to the exhaust manifold, for this was one of founder Cecil Kimber's obsessions.

1932-34 *K3 Magnette*

By 1933, Cecil Kimber had decided that the best possible way of gaining publicity for MG was to see the cars winning motor races. Earlier attempts with four-cylinder types had been successful, but only on a 'class' basis. Now, he concluded, it was time to build a much faster, more powerful, and more purposeful machine.

Design of a new model, the K3 Magnette, began in 1932, and the first two cars were running at the beginning 1933. These were the first of what would be an extremely exclusive breed of MG, for in the next two years only 33 K3s would be produced.

As ever with a new MG of this vintage, the K3 was a mixture of the well proven and the modern, the established, and the adventurous. The chassis frame – it had a 94.2in/2,393mm wheelbase – was an improved version of that already found under the K2 Magnette road cars, as were the front and rear axles, and the

massive 13in/330mm drum brakes.

The real novelty, however, was in the supercharging of the familiar overhead camshaft six-cylinder engine, and its reduction in size to 1,087cc, for this was done to make the car as competitive as possible in the 1100cc capacity class. The original engines were

Below: *Capt. George Eyston and Count 'Johnny' Lurani, with the MG K3 Magnette in which they won their class of the 1933 Mille Miglia race.*

boosted by a Powerplus supercharger, though in 1934 some cars were also supplied with a Marshall blower instead, and all cars were fitted with the ENV-type of four-speed pre-selector transmission.

Although it was made to look longer by the use of the long wheelbase, the body style was really a further evolution of earlier MGs like the J4 Midget, for the cockpit sides were drastically cut down to allow the driver to flail away with his arms and elbows when controlling slides. There were no doors (the side panels were fixed), and the supercharger itself was mounted up front, ahead of the radiator shell, but covered by a bulbous panel between the front of the chassis members.

The body itself was a narrow, as light and as starkly fitted out as International regulations would allow, and all the K3s were distinguished by the exhaust headers and tail pipe which came out of the near side of the bonnet, and along the flanks. On the original cars, the big 'slab' fuel tank was exposed on the tail, with the spare wheel usually strapped in place behind it, but on later examples the tank tended to be hidden under shapely, light-alloy, panels..

The power output achieved varied with the use to which the cars were put, but when The Autocar described the design and tried out a 'works' competition car, it lapped the Brooklands oval race track at almost 105mph, which suggested a top speed of 108 to 110mph. By any standards, for an 1,100cc car of the early 1930s, this was a phenomenal achievement.

Although the K3 Magnette was never meant to be a flexible, go-anywhere, do-anything road sports car, it was an extremely successful flagship for the marque at this time. Three factory-prepared K3s competed in the 1,000-mile Italian road race, the Mille Miglia, where George Eyston, co-piloted by Count 'Johnny' Lurani, won the 1,100cc class, and shattered all previous speed records.

The greatest achievement of all, however, came in the British Ulster TT event, which was held at the end of the 1933 summer. No less a legendary figure than Tazio Nuvolari was persuaded to race a K3, and his co-driver for that race was the intrepid young MG development engineer, Alec Hounslow.

As every MG enthusiast surely knows, Nuvolari not only broke the class lap record seven times during the afternoon, but he also won the entire event on handicap. In later years Hounslow admitted that he had originally been frightened, but later came to marvel at the Italian maestro's pace, especially in a car which rapidly got through its brakes, and often had to be hurled sideways into corners to scrub off speed.

MILESTONE FACTS

- Design of a new model, the K3 Magnette, began in 1932, and the first two cars were running at the beginning 1933.
- Original engines were boosted by a Powerplus supercharger, though in 1934 some cars were also supplied with a Marshall blower instead, and all cars were fitted with the ENV-type of four-speed pre-selector transmission.
- All the K3s were distinguished by the exhaust manifolding and a tail pipe that came out of the near side of the bonnet, and along the flanks.
- The car lapped Brooklands oval racetrack at almost 105mph, which suggested a top speed of 108 to 110mph. By any standards, for a 1,100cc car of the early 1930s, this was a phenomenal achievement.
- No less a legendary figure than Tazio Nuvolari was persuaded to race a K3, and his co-driver for that race was the intrepid young MG development engineer, Alec Hounslow.
- A more modern equivalent of the K3 would be Ford GT40, for both types were just about practical cars for road use, but unsuitable in almost every easy-to-drive way.

Because the UK retail price set for the K3 in 1933 - £795 – was four times that being asked for the entry-level J2, sales were extremely limited. The K3, in any case, was purpose-built for motor racing. A more modern equivalent, for instance, would be Ford GT40, for both types were practical cars for road use, but unsuitable in almost every easy-to-drive way.

The K3, however, did everything ever asked of it, by being a supremely successfully 1.1-liter racing sports car. It was so capable, and so obviously competitive, that on the rare occasions when some mechanical disaster intervened, or the brakes wilted (which they often did), or the driver put one off the road, it caused a real stir. By this time, in fact, Cecil Kimber had discovered that success in motor racing by great cars came to be expected, and any failures hit hard at the perceived image.

Two extra special derivatives of the K3 – one with an offset body for Ronnie Jensen, the other as the 'EX135' project race/record car for George Eyston – both perpetuated the legend yet further. In their original lives, both were successful race cars (EX135 won the British Empire trophy in 1934), but from 1935 the elements of both these machines were combined, a super-streamlined body was devised, and EX135 became the most famous of all MG's record cars. It is preserved, to this day, in the BMIHT collection at Gaydon, in Warwickshire.

(Above) Function, not style, was all important to the K3's dash layout.

(Above left) The K3 Magnette featured a snap-action fuel filler cap.

(Left) Every detail of the K3 Magnette's front suspension and structure was on show.

The free-flow exhaust manifold of the K3 Magnette swept out through the side of the bodywork.

SPECIFICATIONS

Production: 33

Body styles: Open two-seater

Construction: Steel chassis, wood and aluminum body

Engine: Six-cylinders, 1,087cc.

Power Output: Depending on race application

Transmission: Four-speed manual

Suspension: Front – beam axle, leaf springs, rear - beam axle, leaf springs

Brakes: Front drums, rear drums

Maximum speed: 108 mph (174 km/h)

A single SU Carburettor fed the supercharger, which was mounted up front, under and ahead of the water radiator.

1933-34 *L-Type Magna*

Every time MG introduced a new sports car in the early 1930s, they learned as much as possible from the older machines, and re-used as much engineering as possible. Accordingly, when MG enthusiasts got to know about the launch of the L-Type Magna, they knew that there would be similarities with the original F-Type Magnas and the K-Type Magnettes.

The style of the new cars – as usual there was a choice of open and closed examples – was as delicious as ever, for the open two-seater took up elements of the existing J2 (four cylinder) and K-Type Magnette (six-cylinder). No-one could ever confuse such an MG with any other make of British sports car, for the proud, vertical, radiator shell, the slab rear fuel tank complete with its built-on contents gauge, and the sweeping line of the front wings were all typical Abingdon 'trade marks'.

Under these bodies was the latest version of the long-wheelbase (94.2in/2,393mm) chassis, and the long-established 42in./1,067mm front and rear axles, with 12in. diameter drum brakes. This time the six-cylinder engine was a 1,087cc unit (in some ways similar to that of the K3 Magnette power unit), though it was normally aspirated, with twin semi-down-draught SU carburetors, and it produced only 41bhp.

L1 types had four-seater styles, while the L2s had two-seater open styling. Although prices were significantly higher than those of earlier Magnas (the L2 cost £285), these were very popular, and sold well. Not only were these the sturdiest and most versatile six-cylinder MGs yet put on sale, but the 1.1-liter engine was robust enough to withstand considerable power-tuning.

This was a period when Abingdon was often accused, rightly, of playing 'mechanical Meccano' with its engines, chassis and body styles, yet the L-Type Magnas certainly seemed to pick the most attractive, and the most practical of everything that was available at MG. Almost immediately, MG began to sell 10 or 15 L-Types every week, not as many as the F-Type had achieved, but very satisfactory when these cars were also lined up against the popular little J1 and J2 Midgets.

Life behind the wheel of an L-Type was always fun, if cramped and (by later standards) rather cramped, though in this case the presence of a softly-tuned, but smooth, six-cylinder engine helped a lot. The driver and passenger both sat low, with their legs stuck out alongside the transmission. So simple was the bodywork that when the centrally hinged hood panels were lifted up the passengers legs were exposed. Between the cockpit and the engine bay there was only a single sheet of aluminum, while the steering column (right-hand steering only, of course) ran straight from the wheel to the steering box close to the forged front axle beam.

In 1933 The Autocar greeted the latest L-Type Magna by writing these breathless words;

Below: *The L-Type Magna of 1933 was a faster, better-equipped, and up-dated derivative of the original Magna pedigree.*

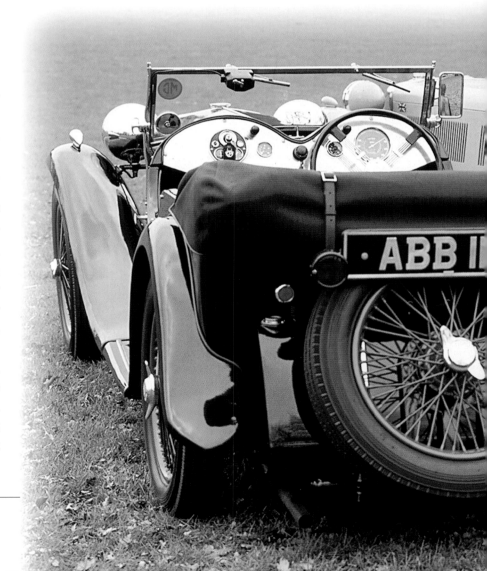

There is a great fascination in driving the Magna. The steering is light and quick – at first grasp disconcertingly so – with a strong caster action, but, as soon as it is realised that the wheel is best held with a light grip, the car can be placed neatly, or taken round curves at speeds, in an elegant manner. Although the car is light and lively, the steering has no apparent vices such as incipient wheel tramp, and the radiator and head lamps do not dither about on bad surfaces. Because of the low build and special form of spring anchorages, the car holds the road excellently.

Taken all round, the open two-seater Magna is a most delectable car with the manners, as well as the air, of a thoroughbred.'

All of the above has to be read with an eye to the standards of the day, for there is no doubt that the Magna, like the Midgets and Magnettes to which it was so closely related, was very hard-sprung, would jump from bump to bump like a mountain goat, and was equipped with very direct steering which needed to learnt, and respected.

MILESTONE FACTS

- Not only were these the sturdiest and most versatile six-cylinder MGs yet put on sale, but the 1.1-liter engine was robust enough to withstand considerable power tuning.

- No-one could ever confuse such an MG with any other make of British sports car, for the proud, vertical, radiator shell, the slab rear fuel tank complete with its built-on fuel gauge were all typical Abingdon trade marks.

- Life behind the wheel of an L-Type was always fun, if cramped, though in this case the presence of a softly-tuned, but smooth, six-cylinder engine helped a lot.

- So simple was the bodywork that when the centrally hinged hood panels were lifted up the passengers legs were exposed.

- Like many other MG sports cars built at this time, the L-Type Magna was not a long-lived model. Cecil Kimber and his planners could always see ways of juggling styles, engine tunes and model names to keep the pot boiling, and made frequent changes.

For those who did not want to live with the rather sketchy all-weather arrangements (which included a 'build-it-yourself soft-top, and removable side-screens), MG also offered a closed four-seater, the Salonette, for £345. Late in 1933, too, an oddly styled version called the 'Continental Coupe' was also added to the range, but these were very rare.

Like many other MG sports cars built at this time, the L-Type Magna was not a long-lived model. Cecil Kimber and his planners could always see ways of juggling styles, engine tunes and model names to keep the pot boiling, and made frequent changes. It's worth remembering that the original F-Type Magna had only been built for one year, the J1/J2 Midgets were on the market for less than two years – and the L-Type Magna would only be available in 1933 and early 1934.

Economically this made little sense to MG's owner, Sir William Morris, who liked to his cars built for a longer period, and in greater quantities, but MG enthusiasts were not interested in the bottom line – merely in fun, performance, and novelty. When it was current, the L-Type Magna was the fastest of the series-production MG models, could cruise comfortably at more than 65mph, and had an all-out top speed of 75mph.

At Abingdon, however, there always seemed to be another new model, ready to take over from a current favourite. The L-Type Magna, therefore, was short-lived, for in 1934 it was to be replaced by the longer, wider and more powerful N-Type Magnette.

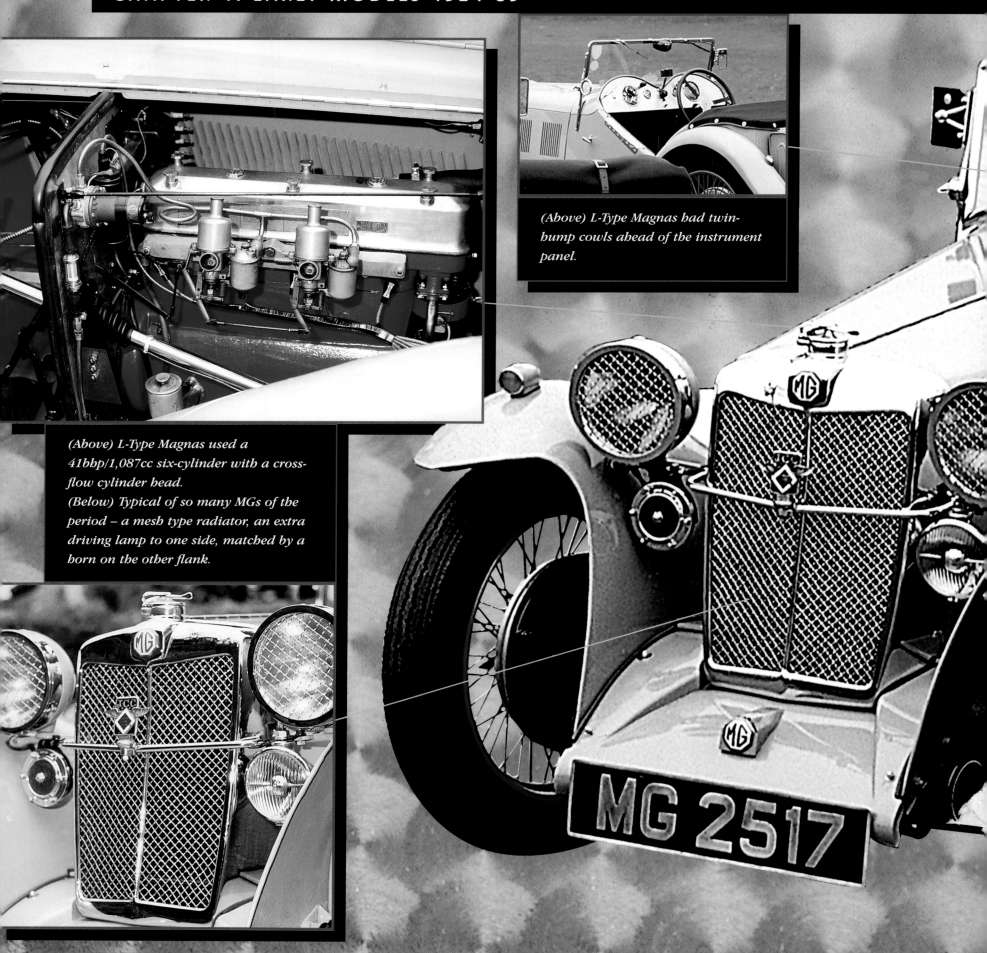

(Above) L-Type Magnas had twin-hump cowls ahead of the instrument panel.

(Above) L-Type Magnas used a 41bhp/1,087cc six-cylinder with a cross-flow cylinder head.
(Below) Typical of so many MGs of the period – a mesh type radiator, an extra driving lamp to one side, matched by a horn on the other flank.

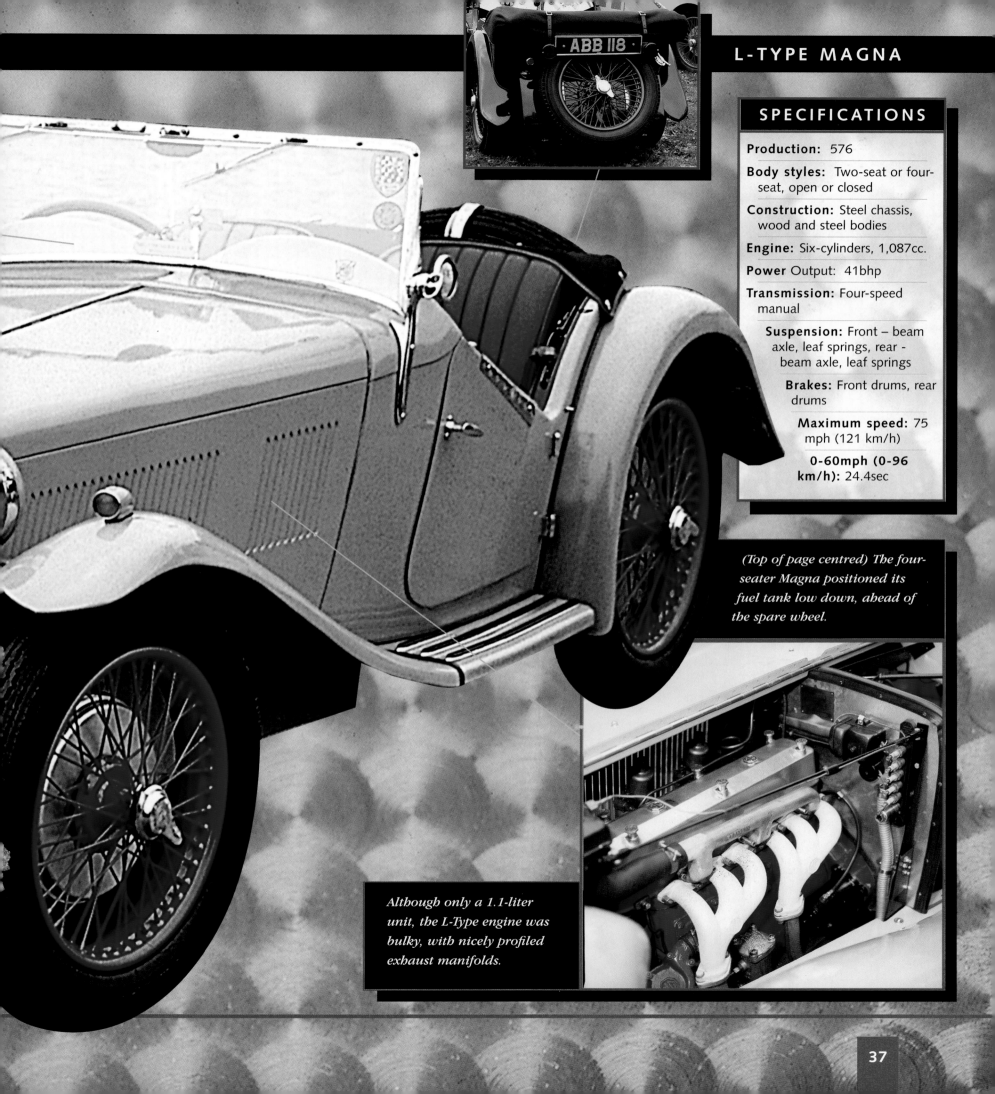

SPECIFICATIONS

Production: 576

Body styles: Two-seat or four-seat, open or closed

Construction: Steel chassis, wood and steel bodies

Engine: Six-cylinders, 1,087cc.

Power Output: 41bhp

Transmission: Four-speed manual

Suspension: Front – beam axle, leaf springs, rear - beam axle, leaf springs

Brakes: Front drums, rear drums

Maximum speed: 75 mph (121 km/h)

0-60mph (0-96 km/h): 24.4sec

(Top of page centred) The four-seater Magna positioned its fuel tank low down, ahead of the spare wheel.

Although only a 1.1-liter unit, the L-Type engine was bulky, with nicely profiled exhaust manifolds.

1934-36 PA AND PB Midget

Less than two years after Abingdon had charmed everyone with the new J2 Midgets, this appealing little car was replaced by yet another new Midget – the P-Type. In many ways this was the best and the most accomplished of all the overhead-camshaft-engined Midgets, for it was also the last to use to use this power unit.

As ever, when a new model was being developed, Cecil Kimber encouraged his engineers to use as many well-proven components as possible. Thus, in the P-Type, elements of the existing J2 and the J4 Midgets were both present, but a great deal of thought had gone into making real improvements. MG, however, made sure that its public would fund their effort, for the new two-seater version of the car cost £220, and the four-seater cost £240.

The P-Type's new chassis frame looked like that of earlier types – the main side members still passed under the line of the rear axle and there was very little cross bracing – but it was much sturdier than before, and the wheelbase dimension had crept up to 87.3in/2,217mm. This stretch was needed to provide enough space in the engine bay, for

there was really very little increase in the passenger cabin, though it was certainly better equipped.

On the other hand, here was a smart little car that looked even more graceful than its immediate predecessor. The general layout and style was the same as before – the MG radiator was unmistakable,

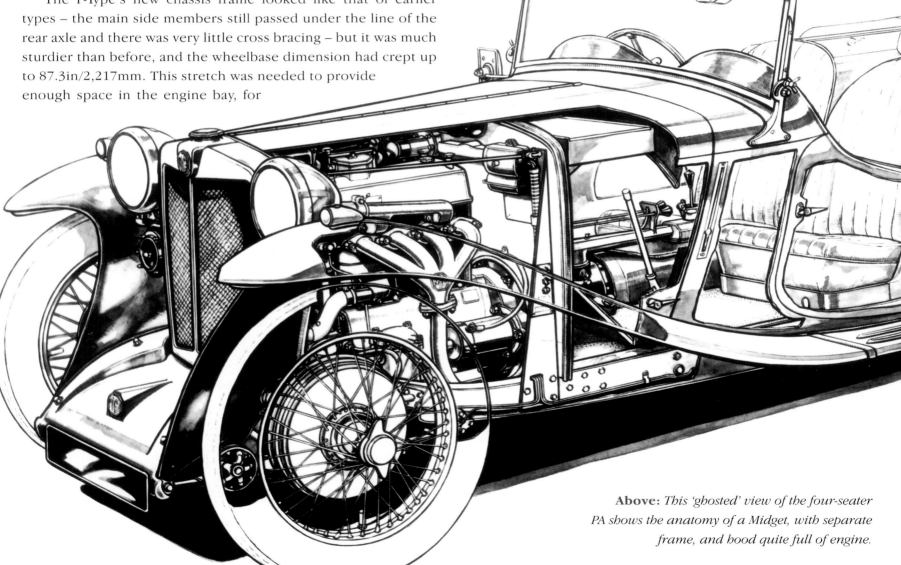

Above: *This 'ghosted' view of the four-seater PA shows the anatomy of a Midget, with separate frame, and hood quite full of engine.*

as were the lines of the wings, the cheeky flares over the tail, the twin humps ahead of the passengers' faces, and the exposed fuel tank on two-seaters – by Cecil Kimber's unerring eye for a line had led to this looking even more seductive.

Mechanically, the most important, hidden improvement, was that the 847cc engine had been thoroughly re-worked, to make it more refined, notably by the use of a three-main-bearing crankshaft. Although smoother than before, there was more internal friction in the latest engine, which was slightly less powerful than the J2 had been – 35bhp instead of 36bhp. On the other hand, the bugbear of crankshafts that broke after persistent over-revving had been banished forever.

Behind the engine, the non-synchromesh gearbox was made stronger than before, as was the rear axle, and to keep the whole car well in check the P-Type was given 12in. diameter drum brakes – this being a real innovation, as all previous road-going Midgets had used 8in. brakes. This all added up to a comprehensive package of improvements, which was greatly to the credit of chief designer Hubert Charles, and his team. They, incidentally, included two notable young men - Syd Enever (who would go on to become MG's Technical Director) and Jack Daniels (who later be closely connected with the Morris Minor and Mini layouts).

Work on improving the layout, the equipment, and the general character of the new car meant that it was significantly heavier than the J2 – in round figures, at the curbside it weighed 1,512lb/686kg instead of 1,260lb/571kg)

The public liked what it saw, so demand for the P-Type took off like a rocket. This smart little car initially sold so well that it supported a general lag in MG sales that was caused by a drop in demand for the six-cylinder types. This was a disappointment to MG, as the N-Type Magnette had been launched at the same time, with a six-cylinder engine, and many shared chassis components.

Slowly but surely, it seemed, MG was turning the Midget into a comfortable touring car, rather than a minimal-motoring two-

seater, for here was a car that could be driven very hard, or used for comfortable touring. It was one that could be entered in reliability trials and tests but also used for holiday transport.

Even so, the clientele soon let it be known that they missed the extra edge of performance. MG worried about this (especially as their biggest rival, Singer, was still making excellent two-seaters), and made haste to offer improvements. From the autumn of 1935, therefore, the P-Type became the PB (and this, automatically, meant that everyone then started calling the earlier type the PA!), with a bored-out version of the engine. The latest unit measured 939cc, and produced 43bhp instead of 35bhp, and came complete with a close-ratio gearbox.

By this time MG had been swept into the Nuffield Organization (previously it had been personally owned by Lord Nuffield), and big changes were on the way, but for the next nine months the PB offered a significantly improved package. In its independent road test, published in January 1936, The Autocar wrote of a 'Fascinating Small Sports Car', noting that it would certainly achieve 75mph or more, and that it was an all-round improvement on the PA that had come before it. The most telling remark was:

'Sometimes the truest expression of opinion … is to say it is a machine one would like to own oneself', which told everyone just how much the team had enjoyed using this car, even in the depths of winter.

The clientele, for sure, agreed with them. Exactly 2,000 PAs had been produced, and 526 of the more powerful PB followed. The TA that took over in 1936 would have an entirely different pedigree.

(Left) Those were the days when car companies spent money on beautifully detailed filler caps.

(Right) Early-type 'Moon' roof on this Airline-bodied P-Type. Nothing's new in motoring, right ?

One the P-Type Airline, these 'Trafficators' were finger indicators to signal a turn.

(Below) No excuse for not knowing what make of sports car this is. Kimber's octagon badges were ever present in the 1930s.

SPECIFICATIONS

Production: 2,000/526

Body styles: Two-seat and four-seat open, and Airline coupe

Construction: Steel chassis, wood and steel bodies

Engine: Four-cylinders, 847cc/939cc.

Power Output: 35/43bhp

Transmission: Four-speed manual

Suspension: Front – beam axle, leaf springs, rear - beam axle, leaf springs

Brakes: Front drums, rear drums

Maximum speed: 74mph (119km/h)/76 mph (122 km/h)

0-60mph (0-96km/h): 32.2/27.4sec

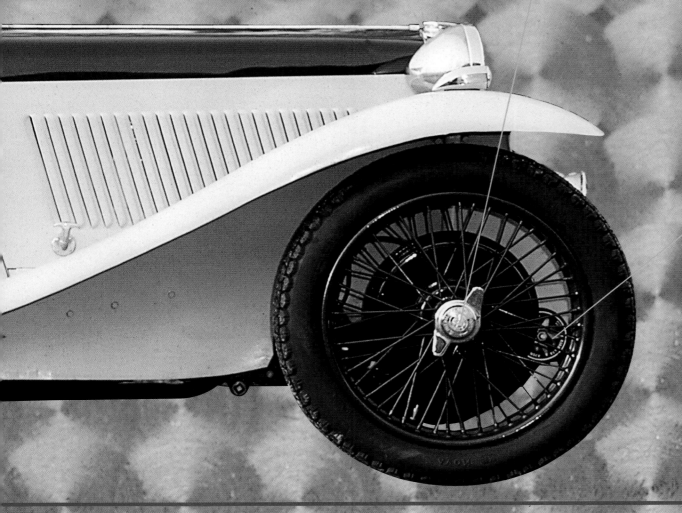

As on so many other MGs of the period, shock absorbing was by lever-arm friction dampers, which could be adjusted to take up the wear.

1934-36 *K Type & KN Magnette*

MG's engineers had been incredibly busy in 1933, for in the spring of 1934 they revealed two important new models. One was the PA Midget, which took over from the much-loved J2, the other being the NA Magnette, which was a direct replacement for the earlier K-Type Magnette.

Even so, there was method in this frenetic activity, for much of the innovative engineering was shared between the new four-cylinder and six-cylinder types.

As with the PA Midget, so with the NA Magnette – MG concentrated on improving, rather than completing changing, the running gear, but the new body style was larger, more spacious, better equipped and somewhat heavier than before. To make sure that they also delivered an improvement in performance, MG also made sure that the six-cylinder was more powerful then ever.

All this had been done logically. To make sure that the new Magnette was, indeed, roomier than before, it had a longer wheelbase and wider wheel tracks. This was the first-ever MG to run on a 96in./2,438mm wheelbase, and the first to use 45in./1,143mm wheel tracks. Most other features of the sturdy new chassis seemed to be familiar, for the new Magnette shared its 12in. drum brakes with those of the PA Midget, although there was a new-type Bishop cam steering box.

Much work had gone into improving the six-cylinder engine, for although it looked superficially similar to those which had gone before (this basic engine had first appeared three years earlier in the F-Type Magna) it was at once more powerful, more robust and more refined.

For the N-Type Magnette, the 1,271cc power unit had a cross-flow cylinder head, and still used twin semi-down-draught SU carburetors, but there were also a pair of splendidly detailed cast iron swept exhaust manifolds. Cylinder head and cylinder block castings were both new, much

attention had finally been given to top-end breathing, and the claimed power output had rocketed to no less than 57bhp.

What was most interesting was the MG had abandoned the pre-selector transmission, which had been a feature of the earlier Magnettes. Even though it made the cars extremely easy to drive (in Britain there were still no compulsory driving tests, and car-makers tried hard to make it as simple as possible for novices to drive their machines), it was heavy, expensive, costly to repair in case of trouble, and had never been popular.

Although such a power figure might sound puny by early twenty-first century standards, it is worth recalling just how far MG had already progressed with this 1,271cc 'six'. The original F-Type Magna engine produced 37bhp, the KD Magnette of late 1933 boasted 49bhp, and now the peak figure was 57bhp. In less than three years, therefore, the rating had been pushed up by no less than 54 per cent. Most of the credit for this went to MG themselves, for although Wolseley was still manufacturing the MG engines, they had little to do with their evolution – and their own derivatives were by no means as effective.

Compared with earlier short-wheelbase Magnettes, and the L-Type Magna, the body styles – two-seater, 2+2-seater, open and closed 'Airline' Coupe – had all grown up a lot, to provide more space. At the front the shell seemed rather more bulky because it had been made a touch higher, the scuttle/firewall was more substantial, and the shells were now mounted on a rubber-insulated sub-frame to

Below: Not all MGs had open-style bodies – this being the close-coupled four-seater with four passenger doors.

cushion them from road and mechanical noises. All cars looked smoother and more refined than before, if only because their fuel tanks were now hidden behind steel panelling in the tail.

Cleverly, MG pitched the prices between those of the L-Type Magna and the early K-Type Magnettes, for the two-seater was to cost £305, and the four-seater tourer £335. Once MG enthusiasts found that the new Magnettes not only looked good, but were also faster than before – a 0-60mph sprint in 22.8seconds was decidedly brisk for the period, and not many British sports cars in this market sector could reach 80mph.

In general, testers' comments were not merely that here was a faster car, but one that felt better developed, and altogether more

versatile. It would be many years before an MG sports car was anything but a wind-in-the hair machine, but this Magnette at least provided that sensation in more style than any previous MG. The public thought so too – for no fewer than 738 of these cars would be sold before assembly ended in 1936.

MG, of course, could never be persuaded to leave a good design alone. Taking lessons from General Motors, no doubt, they believed in mixing and matching wherever possible. Accordingly, from mid-1934 they introduced another derivative of this new type, the KN Magnette, which was by no means as sporting, but still had its own character. The wheelbase had crept up to 108in/2,743mm, and the wheel tracks to 48in/1,220mm, and although the engine was unchanged, this time it had to cope with a more bulky four-seater car body style, which was an updated version of that offered on earlier K-Types.

Although it was only on sale for two seasons, and was priced at £399, MG sold 201 such KNs. It then gave way to the new, and much larger, SA '2-Liter', which was an entirely new type of MG.

Note the combined rev counter/ speedometer in this Magnette – and octagons, of course.

Exposed hinges on the Magnette, not only simple, but giving wider door openings.

Fascinating detail of the passenger door layout on this Magnette.

OV 9919

SPECIFICATIONS

Production: 738/201

Body styles: Two-seat and four-seat sports, four-seat sedan, and Airline coupe

Construction: Steel chassis, wood and steel bodies

Engine: Six- cylinders, 1,271cc.

Power Output: 57bhp

Transmission: Four-speed manual

Suspension: Front – beam axle, leaf springs, rear - beam axle, leaf springs

Brakes: Front drums, rear drums

Maximum speed: 81 mph (130 km/h)

The latest evolution of MG's celebrated overhead-cam six had 57bhp in the 1,271cc KN Magnette.

1936-39 SA '2 LITER'

The first of what we might call the 'Cowley' MGs was the SA, launched in October 1935, though not actually available to customers until March 1936. Designed obediently according to an edict laid down by Nuffield boss Leonard Lord, the SA was by no means as special as the earlier 'overhead-cam' Midgets and Magnettes had been.

Nuffield watchers could see that many of the new car's components had been shared with the latest Wolseley and Morris family cars.

The SA – or the '2-liter' as it was often, quite wrongly, called by MG publicists – was the largest MG so far seen, for it rode on a 123in./3,124mm wheelbase, and had wide, 53.4in/1,356mm wheel tracks. To quote that eminent MG historian, Wilson McComb:

'Gone was the familiar MG chassis; this one was completely conventional in every way. Gone was the ohc engine,: the new one had its overhead valves operated by pushrods. Gone were the cable brakes; the new MG had the Lockheed hydraulic type.'

MG's new owners, the Nuffield Organisation, wanted the new SA to compete, head-on, with cars like the SS-Jaguar 2-Liter, or the Triumph Dolomite. It was no sports car, nor ever meant to be. On the other hand, Nuffield wanted to offer real value, which explains why it was originally priced at just £375

The SA originally revealed was, by no means, the SA, which eventually reached the clientele, for Nuffield's models were changing rapidly at this time, and regular, un-announced, updates were inevitable. The prototype had bolt-on wire wheels, a synchromesh gearbox and a long, direct, gear-shift. By the time sales began, it had been equipped with center-lock wire-spoke wheels, a non-synchromesh gearbox, and a remote-control change. Nor was that all. Only months later a part-synchromesh gearbox was once adapted, while the size of the Wolseley-based engine was pushed up from 2,062cc at launch, to 2,288cc for original customers, then to 2,322cc in the early weeks of 1937.

The style, and the equipment, however, was right, and the customers seemed to enjoy what they were offered. Because this was a large sedan, the body builders – Morris Bodies – could provide a truly elegant four-door shape, which matched up well against its competitors. Before long a two-door Charlesworth tourer, and an extremely elegant drop-head coupe, which was constructed by Tickford, also joined the original sedan. The interior of all these cars was extremely well equipped and, in true Kimber-MG style, the fascia/dashboard display was well laid out and

MILESTONE FACTS

- Designed obediently according to an edict laid down by Nuffield boss Leonard Lord, the SA was by no means as special as the earlier 'overhead-cam' Midgets and Magnettes had been.

- Gone was the familiar MG chassis; this one was completely conventional in every way. Gone was the ohc engine, the new one had its overhead valves operated by pushrods. Gone were the cable brakes; the new MG had the Lockheed hydraulic type.

- It also signaled the intention to keep a popular model in production for some time. Previous MGs, particularly the out-and-out sporty types, had been built for two years, or less, but the SA would remain on the market from March 1936 until the outbreak of war in Europe in September 1939.

- MG's future strategy had become clear. Abingdon might not have abandoned sports cars, but   this, it seemed, was the way they intended to make secure profits in the future.

comprehensive. The fascia board was wood, as were the cappings around all the doors. The seats were leather trimmed, and there were pile carpets on the floor.

The SA, therefore, was aiming to sell in territory, which no previous MG had ever invaded, and seemed to do so very well. MG's own publicists made much of the sporting heritage, and emphasized the continuity of the noble front-end style, and that famous MG octagon badge, while trying to say nothing about this car's obvious relationship to the Wolseley Super Six of the same period. MG dealers (who usually held Morris and Wolseley dealerships within the same premises) did not need to be told, as the close relationship of all the running gear was obvious.

Although these new SAs were by no means as sporting as the little two-seaters for which MG had previously been famous, clearly they tapped into a ready demand, and once parts finally came together in mid-1936, sales and production were brisk. Here was a car which could be cruised at 70mph wherever conditions allowed, with an engine that did not need to be over-revved to deliver that sort of performance, and which no longer needed a specialist mechanic to keep up with it.

Right: *MG assembly at Abingdon in the late 1930s, with TAs closest to the camera, and a line of SA models running parallel to it.*

The chassis, conventional in almost every way, with half-elliptic front and rear springs, with Bishop cam gear steering, and with hydraulic lever-arm dampers at front and rear was intended to deliver comfortable touring, rather than racecar road holding, and delivered on all counts. It was, however, by the far the heaviest MG so far put on sale, at more than 3,300lb/1,497kg, so it could be quite hard work to drive fast, and soon got a reputation for being a handful on slippery surfaces.

Not only was the SA the first of a new breed of MGs, but it also signaled the intention to keep a popular model in production for some time. Previous MGs, particularly the out-and-out sporty types, had been built for two years, or less, but the SA would remain on the market from March 1936 until the outbreak of war, in September 1939.

Naturally it was most popular in 1936 and 1937, when 2,084 of the total production run left the assembly tracks, and by 1939 it had been overcome by the larger-engined WA, which looked similar, but was considerably faster. Most of that total run was of the conventional four-door saloon, while there were only 90 of the Charlesworth Tourers: no fewer than 696 of the supremely elegant Tickford DHC version were sold.

Although many detail changes and improvements were made to the SA in this time, all of them emphasised just how much of a touring, rather than a sporting, car was now being assembled at Abingdon. Once the SA had been joined by the smaller-engined VA (from mid-1937), and by the large, fast and expensive WA in 1938/1939, MG's future strategy had become clear. Abingdon might not have abandoned sports cars, but this, it seemed, was the way they intended to make secure proifits in the future.

Until, that is, Hitler's armies marched in Poland.

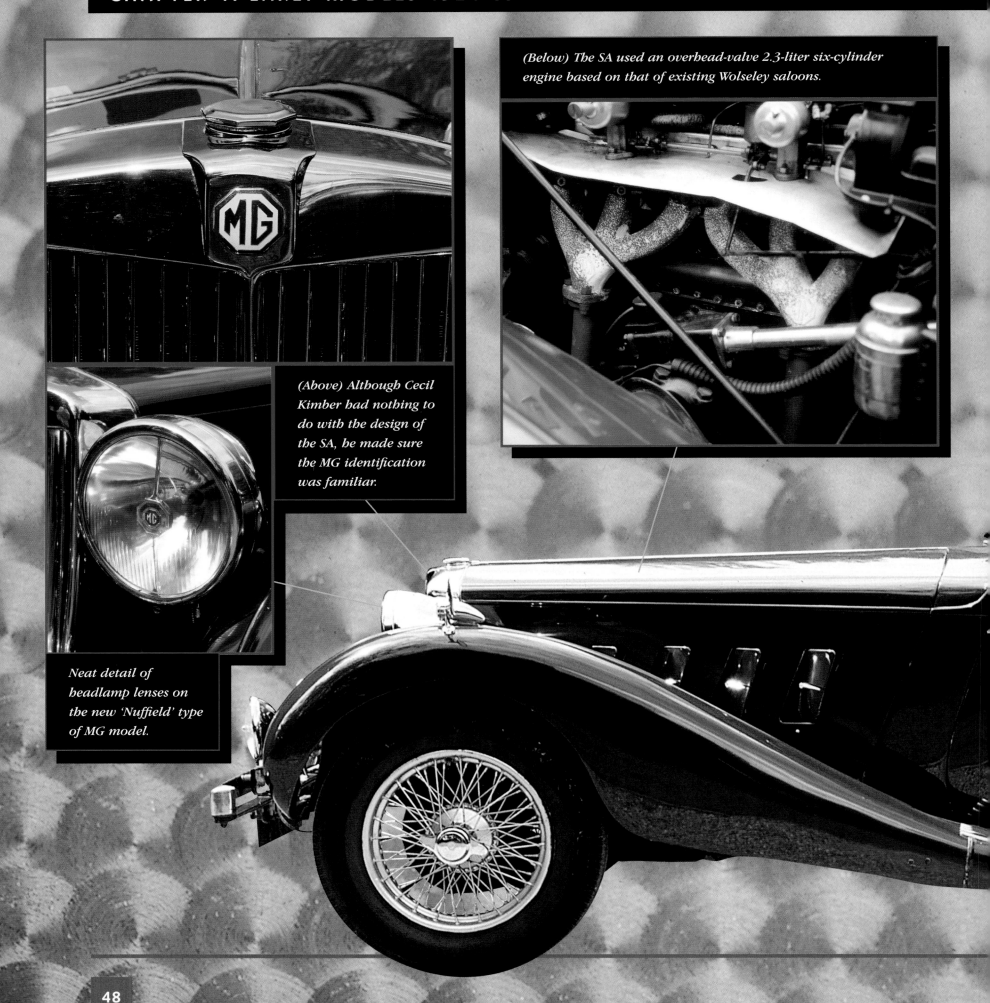

(Below) The SA used an overhead-valve 2.3-liter six-cylinder engine based on that of existing Wolseley saloons.

(Above) Although Cecil Kimber had nothing to do with the design of the SA, he made sure the MG identification was familiar.

Neat detail of headlamp lenses on the new 'Nuffield' type of MG model.

(Below) Simulated gold featured in the SA instrument style, with the clock neatly recessed into the rev-counter dial. (Right) Even on a big car like this, MG persisted with center-lock wire-spoke wheels.

SPECIFICATIONS

Production: 2,738

Body styles: Sedan, tourer, drop-head coupe

Construction: Steel chassis, wood and steel/aluminum bodies

Engine: Six-cylinders, 2,288/2,322cc.

Power Output: 75bhp

Transmission: Four-speed manual

Suspension: Front – beam axle, leaf springs, rear - beam axle, leaf springs

Brakes: Front drums, rear drums

Maximum speed: 85mph (137 km/h)

1936-39 *TA* AND *TB Midget*

Soon after MG became part of the Nuffield Organisation, the engineering staff was moved to Cowley, and instructed to design new models based on cheaper Morris and Wolseley parts. With this in mind, Hubert Charles and Jack Daniels evolved a new Midget – the T-Type – to take over from the much-loved P-Type.

The new car might have been designed at Cowley, incidentally, but it was still to be built on the simple assembly lines at Abingdon.

The original T-Type – later we knew it as the TA – was the first of the new-generation Midgets, which really proved a point for the new management. Although it was different in every way from the PA/PB models – it was larger, heavier, and had a simpler engine – it was also a sales and marketing success. More than this, it laid the foundations for later T-Types, particularly for the post-war TC, which was the first such Midget to be exported to the USA in large numbers.

For the first time since the late 1920s, here was a new Midget, which used no carryover parts from earlier models. Even so, the general layout, style and overall character was preserved – and so was the price, for the original T-Type sold for just £222, which was exactly the same as that of the PB which it replaced. Customers, therefore, never had any difficulty in recognizing one car as a direct successor for the other – though they all had to come to terms with its great bulk, great weight, and altogether different feel on the road.

Although the new chassis layout followed all the long-established Midget traditions – stiff half-elliptic springs, whippy ladder-style chassis frame, narrow cabin and all – the engineering team had made every improvement that they could slip past their paymasters. Here was a Midget with the longest wheelbase yet (it measured 94in/ 2,388mm), and with the largest engine. This was really Magnette territory, and it may be significant that the last Magnettes were produced as the T-Type made its debut. The power unit itself was a modified and up-rated derivative of the existing Wolseley Ten, a simple, old-

Left: *In the late 1930s TA Midgets excelled in that particular British sport of sporting reliability trials. These 'works' assisted cars had lock differentials to give them more traction.*

Above: *The TA chassis layout was similar to that of earlier Midgets, but every detail was different.*

MILESTONE FACTS

- The new car might have been designed at Cowley, incidentally, but it was still to be built on the simple assembly lines at Abingdon.

- Although it was different in every way from the PA/PB models – it was larger, heavier, and had a simpler engine – it was also a sales and marketing success. *

- It laid the foundations for later T-Types, particularly for the post-war TC. The power unit itself was a modified and up-rated derivative of the existing Wolseley Ten, a simple, old-fashioned, long-stroke overhead-valve design, but compared with the old PB it had 52bhp and a lot more torque.

- In all other respects, of course, this was a traditional Midget, for the passengers sat low, the doors were cutaway to increase the elbow- room.

- There was some resistance to the T-Type at first – some die-hards still wanted the overhead-camshaft engines and non-synchromesh transmissions of old – but once the new car's better performance (up to 80mph was possible) became known, demand grew.

fashioned, long-stroke overhead-valve design, but compared with the old PB it had 52bhp and a lot more torque.

The suspension, somehow, was softer than ever before on an MG, which made the car easier to drive on long journeys. Traditionalists were not sure they liked this, at first, but soon realized that they were not tiring as much on hurried journeys. The T-Type, for sure, looked like its predecessors, and behaved in a similar manner, but to produce the same performance the engine did not have to be revved as highly, or the gear shift stirred round quite so often.

In all other respects, of course, this was a traditional Midget, for the passengers sat low, the doors were cutaway to increase the elbow room, and the all-weather protection was simple, clip-on, and usually ignored by any owner until the rain (or snow!) was truly torrential. T-Types had a bench style seat back rest, there was quite a lot of space behind that for stowage (but this was strictly a two-seater) and – as everyone expected – the big fuel tank was exposed on the extreme tail, with wire-spoke spare wheel fixed to that.

Originally, only one body style was available – the traditional-looking MG type of open two-seater roadster, complete with vertical grille, extra driving lamps, and with the front axle and suspension exposed to the onlooker. MGs of this type were still sold without fenders, and the headlamps were still exposed, and mounted one on each side of the radiator.

Shortly afterwards, though, MG announced an alternative to this, which was a smart drop-head coupe derivative, by Tickford. The front-end style was not changed, but aft of the screen the doors were built up and included wind-down glass, while there was a typically-

Tickford drop-head coupe soft top, complete with the curvaceous bars, which supported the mechanism when it was erect. Although these were heavier than the ordinary roadsters, which meant that the fine edge of performance was lost, they were very smart little cars, which became real collectors' pieces in later years.

More than 3,000 such cars would be sold in 30 months, which was a rate MG had never seen before.

Early in 1939, and without making any announcement, MG quietly up-rated the T-Type, into the TB. This was done with no style changes, but by phasing in one major up-date – for the old-type long-stroke 1,292cc engine had been replaced by the new-generation 1,250cc power unit. This was the first that the later-famous XPAG engine was seen in an MG: it was a unit that would also power the Y-Types, the TC, TD and TF models in the next 15 years. As noted so carefully in John Thornley's book Maintaining the Breed, it could be power-tuned, supercharged even, and provide modified MGs with truly outstanding performance.

Because of the outbreak of war in Europe on 3 September 1939, there was little time to build and develop the TB pedigree, so only 379 such cars were ever made. Six years later, and after the fighting was over, MG would resurrect the model, make minor changes to it, call it the TC, and sell a further 10,000 copies.

SPECIFICATIONS

Production: 3,003/379

Body styles: Two-seat sports, Airline coupe, and drop head coupe

Construction: Steel chassis, wood and steel bodies

Engine: Four-cylinders, 1,292cc/1,250cc.

Power Output: 52/54bhp

Transmission: Four-speed manual

Suspension: Front – beam axle, leaf springs, rear - beam axle, leaf springs

Brakes: Front drums, rear drums

Maximum speed: 78 mph (125 km/h)

0-60mph (0-96km/h): 23.1sec/22.7sec

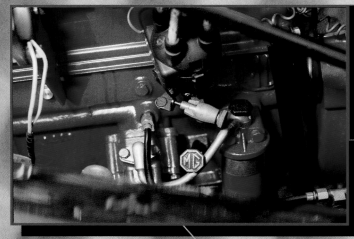

(Left) Distributor/oil filter layout.
(Right) The TA fascia layout always put the speedometer ahead of the passenger's eyes.

MG owners could always find space for maintenance and repairs, for this was a simply constructed car.

(Above) The manufacturer's name featured on this sill plate on the TA model.

(Right) Front end detail, showing the forged axle beam, stiff leaf springs, and lever-arm dampers.

1937-39 VA '1½ LITER'

In 1935, from the very beginning of MG's new regime, Nuffield planned to develop a 'little brother' to the SA. There was a limit to what could be achieved in a hurry, though, and work on the T-Type had to take precedence. Even so, although a new 1.5-liter engined model, the VA (or 'One-and-a-Half Liter') was previewed in October 1936, the first deliveries would not take place until mid-1937.

Here was another new MG whose character was very different from that of the early-1930s MGs. Touring instead of sporting, simple instead of complicated, cheap to build rather than pernickety – and, above all, profitable to the owners – the VA would be yet another success. In little more than two years, mid-1937 to late 1939, no fewer than 2,407 were sold.

Although the VA fitted into MG's line-up where a Magnette had previously lived, it was an entirely different type of car. Magnettes had been all engine – six-cylinder overhead-camshaft engine at that – with restricted passenger space, but the VA was a more spacious model with a humble four-cylinder engine.

Like 'big brother', the SA, the VA's running gear was developed from that of a Wolseley model – this time it was the Wolseley Series II 12/48 – and the engine was effectively just two thirds of the SA's power unit, with four-cylinders instead of six, and was matched by a synchromesh four-speed gearbox from the same model. The 108in/2,743mm wheelbase was just the same as the ousted KN Magnette, but the frame was new, and the wheel tracks had been pushed out to 50in/1,270mm. The SA therefore looked, and was, a very genuine four-seater, and of course it was the first MG model of this size to have four-door coachwork.

Below: *Three body types of SA were made available, this being the popular Tourer from Morris Bodies.*

Morris Bodies provided the four-door sedan body shell (these were built in Coventry), and since MG only asked £325 these proved to be much the most popular. There were, however, two other derivatives, the open four-seater Tourer (£280, from Morris Bodies) and a smart four-seater Tickford-bodied drop-head coupe for £335. The same styling trends had influenced the shaping of the VA, as the SA, and since the two cars had evolved more or less in parallel there were strong visual links between the two.

Unhappily, the VA was not the sporting car than MG would have hoped, for the 1,548cc produced only 54bhp – which was actually less than the power of the 1.3-liter KN Magnette. Within a year a version of this engine would also be fitted to the latest Morris Twelve SIII models. Since the VA was quite a lot heavier than the KN, the car's acceleration could feel positively leisurely at times. As Britain's *Motor* magazine commented when it tested a VA Tourer in 1937:

'If one wanted to term it a sports model, then it would have to be classed with the new regime of silent sports motoring which is becoming so popular.'

Nevertheless, the VA was happy to cruise at up to 70mph where the traffic would allow it, and the famous MG badge certainly helped to maintain a proper image. Major competition came from Riley, Triumph and SS-Jaguar (whose1 ½-liter had a side-valve engine until late 1937), but it was not long before the VA was matching all these cars, sale for sale.

Especially in sedan and drop-head coupe guises, the VA certainly looked the part, for Cecil Kimber had made sure that his influence, especially in decoration, and the use of octagonal MG motifs, was everywhere. Cecil Kimber was proud of this model, and often stated that it was his favorite MG style of the 1930s.Although there were apparently no common panels, the VA and SA were so similarly styled that it was easy enough for one car to be compared with the other. VA owners, if not SA owners, liked that very much.

One attraction of this car was that the chassis specification was very complete, and up-to-the-minute, for there was a telescopically-adjustable steering column, the brakes were hydraulic (by Lockheed), the chassis lubrication nipples were grouped together in the engine bay, and the Luvax lever-type dampers could be adjusted for stiffness from the driver's seat. Jackall jacks, that could lift wheels off the ground without a driver having to grub around in the dirt, were available for

MILESTONE FACTS

- The new 1.5-liter engined model, the VA (or 'One-and-a-Half Liter') was previewed in October 1936, the first deliveries would not take place until mid-1937.

- Like 'big brother', the SA, the VA's running gear was developed from that of a Wolseley model – this time it was the Wolseley Series II 12/48 Nevertheless, the VA was happy to cruise at up to 70mph where the traffic would allow it, and the famous MG badge certainly helped to maintain a proper image.

- Major competition came from Riley, Triumph and SS-Jaguar (whose1½ liter had a side-valve engine until late 1937).

- Unhappily, the VA was not the sporting car than MG would have hoped, for the 1,548cc produced only 54bhp – which was actually less than the power of the 1.3-liter KN Magnette.

- One attraction of this car was that the chassis specification was very complete, and up-to-the-minute, for there was a telescopically-adjustable steering column, the brakes were hydraulic (by Lockheed), the chassis lubrication nipples were grouped together in the engine bay, and the Luvax lever-type dampers could be adjusted for stiffness from the driver's seat.

a mere £5 extra – many VA had them fitted.

Although MG owners originally complained about the very conventional specification of the overhead-valve engine, they learned to love it, for a similar (though smaller in capacity) version was already been fitted to the T-Type sports car, and super-tuned versions of 1.7-liter were sometimes used in 'works' trials cars.

Here was a car that succeeded in spite of the media's generally rather lukewarm response to it. The public, especially the British middle-class clientele who were still not very prosperous (the Depression had only been out of the way for four years), and were looking for value for money, an established image, and were willing to give up a bit of excitement for that.

This explains, for sure, why VA production at Abingdon soon settled down to between 60 and 80 cars a week, which made this the most popular MG 'tourer' of the period. Factory pictures usually show that the assembly lines were well stocked with Vas and T-Types, but that the larger (and more costly) SA was less obvious.

Sales fell away in 1939 (only 447 VAs were produced in that year), but it was the last car to remain production when the decks were being cleared to make way for military machinery to be produced. However, like the SA and the WA, this car would not be re-introduced after that war had been won.

(Left) The VA fascia was well-loaded with instruments, all mounted in a wooden dashboard. On this sedan the central lever controls opening and closing of the windscreen.

(Right) The 1,548cc engine of the VA was an overhead-valve design, a very close relative to the 1,292cc power unit also used in the MG TA sports car.

Not much luggage space on this VA sedan, but still a great advance on previous small MG models.

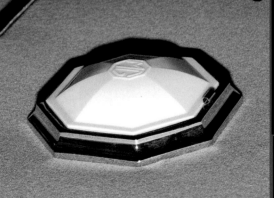

(Let)The Kimber styling influence was ever-present, even on the VA, with this octagon motif.

A headache for today's restorer would be to replicate the badge and glass pattern of this VA headlamp.

SPECIFICATIONS

Production: 2,407

Body styles: Sedan, tourer, drop-head coupe

Construction: Steel chassis, wood and steel bodies

Engine: Four-cylinders, 1,548cc.

Power Output: 54bhp

Transmission: Four-speed manual

Suspension: Front – beam axle, leaf springs, rear - beam axle, leaf springs

Brakes: Front drums, rear drums

Maximum speed: 75mph (121 km/h)

0-60mph (0-96 km/h): 38secs

BJU 606

1938-39 WA '2.6 LITER'

MG's last pre-war car, the WA, was also the largest it had ever made. Spurred on by their success in selling SA and VA models, Nuffield decided to complete the re-alignment by evolving a new, large, six-cylinder car, with which to fight the SS-Jaguar saloon range head on.

In marketing terms, it was about as far away from the T-Type Midget as possible – but it was also very luxuriously trimmed, equipped, and specified. Except for the MG's out-and-out racecars, this was also the fastest MG yet put on sale.

There is no doubt that MG wanted to meet the big Jaguars, head-on, for this was a market where they could see a lot of profitable sales being made. Accordingly, Hubert Charles's team was encouraged to produce a new car by stretching the SA's engineering, by dipping in to the Wolseley parts bin, and by altering SA body styles without spending a fortune on new tooling. This was the theory, but by the time the new car went on the market, most components had been beefed up, modified, or actually renewed – and the car weighed 300lb/136kg more than the equivalent SA.

Working cleverly within these constraints, the team produced an appealing, if larger, heavier and more costly range. Because all private car assembly ended in the autumn of 1939, WA sales had little time to get established. This, and the starting price of £442 (which was more than that of the SS-Jaguar 2½-liter by which MG measured itself) held down sales to only 369, but the new model's smooth, long-legged reputation was beginning to spread by that time.

Although the WA used the same basic chassis frame as the SA, it was modified towards the rear, and the rear tread dimension went up by 3.4in/86mm. The same suspension, steering and mechanical layout was maintained, though the brakes were enlarged to a positively gargantuan 14in/356mm in diameter. This time the hydraulically operated Jackall jacks, front and rear,

were standard. The secret to the WA's performance, however, was that an enlarged version of the VA's engine was fitted, this being a 2,561cc six-cylinder power unit which produced 96bhp: this compared with the 2,322cc/75bhp of the existing SA model.

At Kimber's insistence, changes were made to the styling of all three body-derivatives – the sedan, tourer and drop-head coupe types all came from the familiar SA suppliers. The spare wheel was no longer hooked up at the rear, but was recessed into the left-side front wing, the rear-end styles were more flowing because of this, and rear fenders were fitted. Rear door profiles and the rear quarters of the shell were also modified; one would have expected to find a wider rear seat, but the existing SA type of seating was retained.

At the front, the radiator was further forward than before (though the larger-capacity engine was no longer, nor any more bulky) and had a definite V-profile, while the sweep of the front wings had also been altered. Students of body design will realize that all this must have meant a wholesale carve-up of tooling,

Here was the biggest, the most handsome, and certainly the fastest MG road car so far offered. Saloons were priced at £442, the very rare Tourer at £450, and the outstandingly elegant Tickford-bodied DHC at £468. To this who might otherwise be going to buy an SS Jaguar or (rarer, these people) a six-cylinder engined Triumph Dolomite, these prices were stiff, but not unreasonable.

Independent road tests flagged up a top speed of between 90mph and 94mph, which

Below: *When introduced in 1938, the WA was the largest MG ever to be put on sale.*

meant that the WA was real competition for the SS-Jaguars. In those days, remember, it was only cars like the V12-engined Lagonda which could reach 100mph, for even the best and latest Bentleys of the period were all out at 95mph.

0-50mph in 10.4sec, and 0-60mph in about 14.5sec, were both outstanding brisk for this period – so it was no wonder that enthusiasts soon began to respect the WA, nor was it at all surprising to note that some filtered in British police forces for use as 'chase' cars.

But it was not just the performance, which sold the WA to its

restricted number of clients. Inside, and even more so than the SA, it was an extremely well equipped machine. Compared with the SA, the fascia/instrument panel layout was all new, for (Cecil Kimber must have loved this) the four major instrument bezels had octagon-styled surrounds, and had been raised to be more in line with the driver's eyes.

This, no question, was the last of the line, for the MG pedigree in general was beginning to look 'traditional' which, to cynics, meant that it was slightly old-fashioned. More and more of MG's competitors were beginning to adopt independent front suspension, SS-Jaguar would even offer a heater for its still-born 1940 models, and styling trends were certainly about to bury headlamps into the sheet metal.

The WA, therefore, could be described as distinctive, noble, typically-MG, and praised for its high-speed cruising potential, but there was no doubt that it would have to be modernized, or replaced, in short order for MG to stay abreast of its competition.

In calendar year 1939, MG built 314 WAs, along with 128 SAs and 447 VAs, - their production rate at Abingdon was just two thirds of that achieved in 1938, though one reason for this was that the government had recently raised motor taxation to pay for re-armament. They will all go down in history, however, as the models, which successfully bridged the gap between the early, specialist, MGs, and the enlarged MG operation which would follow in 1945.

(Left) The interior of the WA
was luxuriously equipped,
featuring high-quality trim
materials to match what was
then being offered by SS-Jaguar.
(Right) Knock-off hub spinners
and center-lock wire wheels
were standard on the WA.

(Right) When asked to pay £442 for the WA in 1938/1939, customers had every right to expect very carefully detailed and styled features – such as this in-laid wood capping on the interior.

SPECIFICATIONS

Production: 369

Body styles: Sedan, tourer and drop-head coupe

Construction: Steel chassis, wood and steel bodies

Engine: Six-cylinders, 2,561cc.

Power Output: 96bhp

Transmission: Four-speed manual

Suspension: Front – beam axle, leaf springs, rear - beam axle, leaf springs

Brakes: Front drums, rear drums

Maximum speed: 91mph (146 km/h)

0-60mph (0-96 km/h): 14.5sec

Styling had advanced remarkably in the late 1930s, so the WA had a divided rear window, but the spare wheel had now been relocated to the front wing, with the rear end of the body now much smoother than before.

(Left) The WA was equipped with on-board hydraulic jacks, which was an advanced feature for its day.

FOE 524

1945-49 TC Midget

Almost as soon as the war was won, MG cleared out its factory at Abingdon, dug the sports car tooling out of store, and prepared to begin building private cars once again. In the aftermath of war there were serious material shortages.

Because the government needed to recoup as much hard currency as possible, its new policy was to allocate sheet steel supplied only to those car makers which would export most of their output.

Until 1939 MG had sold most of its cars at home, but from 1945, at a stroke, it was obliged to find overseas markets for its products. Fortunately, many Allied servicemen (particularly Americans) who had been based in the UK in the later stages of the war, had often seen, driven and fallen in love with MG sports cars. When they got home, a demand was almost assured.

With that in mind MG looked at their most modern sports car, the TB of 1939, updated it where appropriate, and put the revised model, the TC, into production. Mechanically, the TC was almost identical with the TB, and certainly it looked the same, though the development engineers did what they could to make improvements.

Almost every aspect of the TB was carried forward to the TC, but there were two important changes. One was that the width of the passenger cockpit was increased by a claimed four inches (to give that important bit extra elbow room), and the other was that

conventional leaf spring shackles replaced the sliding trunnions which had been a feature of the pre-war TB model.

As a matter of policy, and of expediency (for getting the cars back into production was an important consideration) it was decided that there should only be one type of TC, that being the two-seater Roadster, whose body shell would come from Morris Bodies in Coventry. Although the Tickford drop-head coupe alternative style of TA and TB had been well-received, it had not sold in big numbers (only 260 TA Tickfords had been produced, and very few TB Tickford types), so it was never re-introduced..

The assembly tracks took only weeks to be re-installed at Abingdon, which meant that the very first TC production car was pushed off the end of the tracks on 17 September 1945. Thereafter, production built up as rapidly as possible, the limit always being the supply of major components, not least the chassis frames and the body shells.

Although the TC was immediately given a British retail price, there was only limited supply for British customers at first, for many were going for export. Between 1939 and 1945 there had been a huge price increase, not only because of the inflation which occurred during the war years, but because British Purchase Tax now applied, at the rate of 33⅓%.. In 1939, a TB cost £225, and in 1945/1946 a TC was priced at £480, which was a 213 per cent increase – and there would be more increases to follow.

Immediately after the war, there seemed to be an insatiable demand for new cars, all over the world. Once the word got around that the TC was available, demand took off like a rocket. Early in 1946, TCs were already being built at the rate of 110 to 120 cars a month, and by the end of that year

Left: *The TC took over from the TB in post-war Britain. This, too, was the clothing which was fashionable in the late 1940s.*

Abingdon was busier, and making more cars, than it had ever been in the 1930s – and all of them were of this one model. By 1947 that monthly rate had been pushed up further, to 150 or 160 cars every month.

Although GI Joe took home many happy wartime memories of the MG Midgets, he could not actually buy one in the USA at first, where official sales did not begin until the end of 1947. Even then he had to make do with right-hand steering: not that this mattered all that much, for the TC, like its predecessors, was a slim car. Despite its throwbacks to the past, for there was so much post-war joie de vivre in the air that customers could forgive it everything. No independent front suspension? So what. A hard ride? That's what a sports car should feel like surely? No heater? Who needed a heater? Water leaked into the cabin during heavy rain? Yes, just as it had always done in a sports car.

The British motoring press, still very definitely 'on side' as far as UK cars were concerned, always gave the TC an easy ride, though by 1949, when it had already been on sale for four years, criticism of the old-fashioned chassis began to mount.

The Autocar wrote that : 'Today it is certainly a class alone among cars made anywhere in the world', but it then went on to state that: 'The merits and demerits of normal versus independent suspension can be argued, in the main to the latter's marked advantage, but there is no doubt of one fact … that the normally sprung car, rather hard sprung, as in this case, does let the driver gauge within close limits the speed at which he can corner safely fast ….'

Before the last TC of all – the last beam-front-axle MG of all, as it happened – was produced at the end of 1949, MG had built no fewer than 10,000 such cars, which was by far the highest figure yet achieved by this bustling little business. It would need an even better sports car to beat that achievement – and the TD would do the trick.

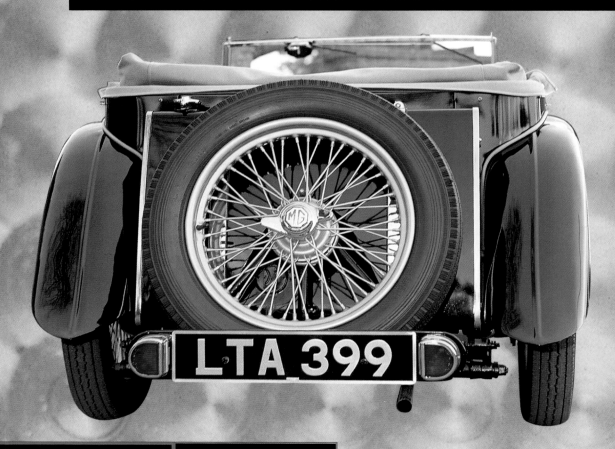

The TC's engine, first seen on the TB of 1939, was the celebrated overhead-valve 'XPAG' type.

(Left) Still fashionable in the late 1940s, the Lucas sidelamps still had discreet little Lucas badges on their chrome covers.

Neatly packaged, to squeeze everything under the bonnet, the TC carried its air cleaner between the SU carburetors.

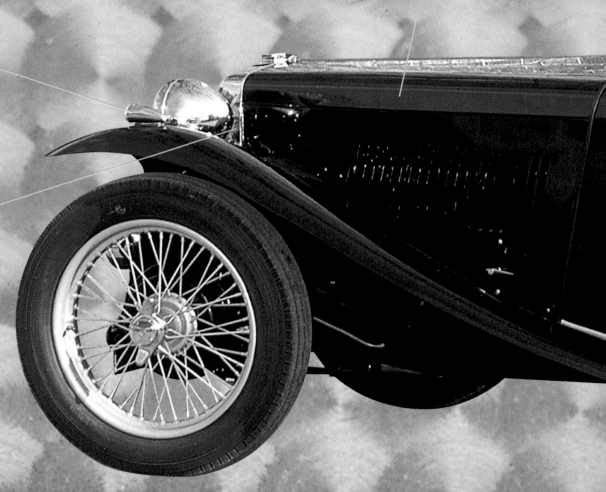

As if by tradition, the TC's speedometer was placed ahead of the co-driver/passenger's eye line. (Right) The TC's slab fuel tank was exposed at the rear, with a snap-action filler cap.

SPECIFICATIONS

Model: TC Midget

Production: 10,000

Body styles: Two-seater sports

Construction: Steel chassis, wood and steel body

Engine: Four-cylinders, 1,250cc.

Power Output: 54bhp

Transmission: Four-speed manual

Suspension: Front – beam axle, leaf springs, rear - beam axle, leaf springs

Brakes: Front drums, rear drums

Maximum speed: 75mph (121 km/h)

0-60mph (0-96 km/h): 22.7sec

1947-53 YA 1¼ LITER SALOON

In the late 1930s, Nuffield's master plan for MG visualised a complete range of sedan models with which to fight other cars targeted at the better off motorist. By 1939 the SA, VW and WA types had already been put on sale, and if the 1939 – 1945 war had not intervened, they would surely have been joined by the Y-Type. We now know that it was originally scheduled for launch in 1940.

As it was this, the smallest MG sedan of the period, could not be put on sale until 1947, by which time the first prototype had put in an enormous test mileage for the company as essential war-time transportation. Like other contemporary MGs, the Y-Type was solidly based on modern Morris and Wolseley engineering, which reduced MG's production and investment costs considerably.

At a casual glance this was merely an appealing, but not very fast, four-door sedan, graced by a de-tuned version of the TC's 1,250cc engine, and carrying that proud MG grille and octagon badge. It was, however, a very significant model in several ways.

Notably it was the first-ever MG to be fitted with independent front suspension, and the very first to be fitted with rack-and-pinion steering. It was also the first to be fitted with a body shell from the newly-established Nuffield Metal Products business, of Birmingham, and the first to be sold exclusively with pressed steel disc wheels, but this was done for cost reasons, rather than for any engineering reason. But there was more than this – it was also a considerable up-grade of the small Morris/Wolseley models on which it was based, yet in the end they were never treated to such innovations.

Not only that, but the modern front suspension/steering installation had originally been designed in 1938-1939 by a young man called Alec Issigonis. Although he was neither senior, not well known, at Cowley (where all MGs were then being engineered) he was seen as a rising star, with very advanced, clearly successful ideas. The front-end package which he evolved might also have been fitted to a modern small Wolseley, but not to the equivalent Morris as it was considered too expensive.

The truly important significance of this piece of mechanical kit was that in one form or another, modified, reinforced and up-dated, in future years it would be also used in the YT, TD, TF, MGA, MGB, MGB GT V8 and RV8 models. Featuring coil springs, lower wishbones, and a lever arm hydraulic damper whose link also doubled as an upper wishbone, it was a true space-saving classic, which melded perfectly with the slim-line, and inch-accurate, rack-and-pinion steering gear.

The structure was an interesting up-date of the four-door Morris

MILESTONE FACTS

- The YA was the first post-war MG sedan
- The YA was the first-ever all-steel-bodied MG model
- The YA was the first MG sedan to be based on a Morris model.
- The YA was the first series production MG to use independent front suspension
- Alec Issigonis, later famous for his Mini design, had engineered the front suspension.

Eight Series E which had been launched in 1938. Whereas that car had a flat head engine of no great merit, the Y-Type was fitted with a 46bhp version of the TC's power unit, the rear of the body shell was given more sweeping and graceful lines, and the nose, naturally, was longer, and had an MG radiator shell up front. The chassis frame itself had sturdily engineered box-section side members and, as was traditional on MGs of this period, passed under the line of the rear axle.

Although critics immediately suggested that the Y-Type was over-engineered, and that the chassis could deal with much more than the 46bhp provided, was a likeable and capable machine, Although it was, indeed, not very fast – the top speed was little more than 70mph – it handled like no previous MG had ever done (in fact there was a tendency to oversteer, at this stage in its life), for the ride was much softer, and the steering felt so much precise. Except for the lack pf pace, here was a true prototype of MG sports cars which would follow – especially of the TD, which was directly evolved from the Y-Type.

A measure of its charm is that a noted MG historian, Anders Clausager, later labelled it 'Sweetness and Light'. In character, in fittings, in its background, and in the manner of its delivery, it lived up to its price which, because of post-war inflation, had to be no less than £672. It was a car which MG soon found that they could export in numbers, with right-hand steering exports almost matching those deliveries made to British customers. In the early months, in fact, most Y-Types were produced for export markets, which ensured the company adequate steel supplies to continue in the private car business. The Y-Type, incidentally, was also the very first MG to be put on sale with left-hand steering, though only 327 such cars were ever produced.

Soon after launch, MG also decided to produce an open-top derivative of this car, which became the YT, and was only ever sold overseas. This is described on page 70.

Late in 1951 Abingdon brought in a revised, and somewhat modernised, version of this car, which therefore became known as the YB. Although the style and general layout was not changed, and the engine specification was not changed, the YB had an improved chassis which used the smaller road wheels of the TD Midget (which, by that time, was in production, the two-leading shoe drum brake installation of that model, plus a front suspension anti-sway bar, and a hypoid-bevel (instead of spiral-bevel) rear axle. The handling was more predictable than before, and this up-dating package kept the Y-Series alive for two more years (for the YT Tourer had not been a success) and a total of 1,301 such sedans were sold.

The successor to this fine, if rather old-fashioned car, was the YA Magnette of 1953.

Below: *The Y-Type was the only MG sedan to be built at Abingdon in the late 1940s, and was the first all-steel body shell to carry the MG badge.*

SPECIFICATIONS

Production:
6,158(YA)/1,301(YB)

Body styles: Four-door sedan

Construction: Steel chassis, steel body

Engine: Four-cylinders, 1,250cc.

Power Output: 46bhp

Transmission: Four-speed manual

Suspension: Front – independent, coil springs, rear - beam axle, leaf springs

Brakes: Front drums, rear drums

Maximum speed: 71 mph (114 km/h)

0-60mph (0-96 km/h): 28.2sec

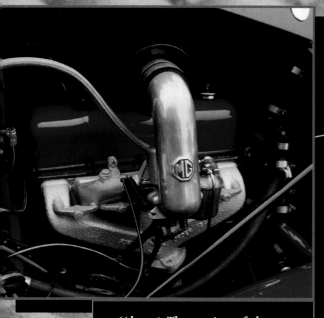

(Above) The engine of the original Y-Type was a de-tuned version of that used in the TC sports car.
(Top Right)One charming pre-war-type feature of the Y-Type was the openable windscreen.

(Abovr) On the Y-Type, as on every other MG of the period, the famous octagon was in evidence.
(Top) In style the Y-Type was much like the larger WA of 1938-1939.

Almost every under-bonnet detail of the Y-Type confirms that it was originally engineered in the late 1930s.

PRB 346

1948-50 YT Tourer

The Y-Type sedan had only been on sale for a few months when MG's management decided that they should also add a convertible version of this car to the range. However, because the Y-Type used a pressed-steel body shell, which was constructed on complex and expensive (for the period) machinery, it meant that this was not going to be easy.

Accordingly, for a new model which they called YT (T = Tourer), MG reverted to traditional body-construction methods, of building up a body shell on a simple wood (mainly ash) framed skeleton. At the time same time, they decided that although the new type would have only two passenger doors, it would still be a four-seater. The resulting YT was seen for the first time in the autumn of 1948, and would be produced in limited numbers for the next two years.

As the YT was always intended as an Export-Only model – surviving Chassis records show that no car was ever officially sold to a UK-based customer – MG decided to give it more power than the sedan. Accordingly, the same engine as currently used in the TC sports car was fitted, which developed 54bhp instead of the 46bhp of the Y-Type sedan. This was wise, in any case, as the YT certainly had less favourable aerodynamics than the sedan so more power was needed to combat more drag, to get the same result.

Although the YT was closely based on the engineering of the Y-Type, it had its very own character, and its own idiosyncrasies. Although the front end style was exactly like that of the Y-Type saloon, the main centre/rear section of the body shell was unique, and had very different proportions. Some artistic observers, indeed, likened it to the same sort of style as had been used on VA and SA types of the late 1930s.

Although the twin-SU-carbureted engine was that of the TC sports car, under the skin, the remainder of the rolling chassis was the same as that of the Y-Type sedan. This, therefore, became the second MG to use coil spring independent front suspension, and rack-and-pinion steering.

By 1948 standards the body, its style, its construction, and its general chunky appeal, was a real throw-back to the 1930s. Up front the pressings, the flowing line of the front wings and the valances, were all identical to those of the Y-Type sedan, but from the bulkhead backwards they were new – and looking old-fashioned.

Not only were there only two passenger doors, but they were hinged at the rear (nowadays we might scathingly call them 'suicide' doors). The pressings of the doors themselves were heavily cut away at elbow height, just as in pre-war MGs, which ensured that wind-down window glass could not be provided. In fact the YT was provided with a traditional type of fold-flat windshield, with removable plastic side screens, and a rather bulky (though un-padded) fold-back soft top hood. Immediately behind the windshield the scuttle

Left: *Based on the Y-Type chassis, the YT Tourer was intended purely for sale into export markets. Compared with the Y-Type saloon, the YT used a more powerful, TC-rated, engine.*

MILESTONE FACTS

- The YT model was built for export only. Officially, no YT was ever delivered to a buyer in Britain.
- Mechanically, the YT was closely based on the YA sedan
- YT bodies used the front end of a YA shell, but with a traditional four seater tourer section
- The YT shared exactly the same engine as the TC sports car
- Only 877 YTs were produced. By post-war Abingdon standards, this made it a rarity.

featured two humps in front of the passengers' faces – another visual throw-back to T-Type sports cars, and the wooden fascia featured TC instruments, where the speedometer was on the passenger's side, and the rev-counter ahead of the driver's eyes.

If this sounds like an amalgam of ideas, in construction it was precisely that. Nuffield Metal Products of Birmingham (who built the Y-Type sedan shell) provided many front end and floor pressings for the YT, but delivered these to Morris Bodies of Coventry, who then constructed the rest of the shell, before delivering the still incomplete assembly to MG at Abingdon, where final completion and assembly took place.

In almost every way, therefore, MG intended this to be thought of as a four seater sports car. Unhappily for the YT's image, however, it was rather too heavy to provide exhilarating performance, so customers could get their enjoyment only from the simple, easy to manage, breeze-in-the-face character of this tourer.

Although MG would dearly have wished to sell many of these tourers to the USA, the YT was not really fast enough, or stylish enough, to appeal to the US market's many sporty-minded drivers .Accordingly, and even though this was definitely an 'Export Only' model, only 161 YTs were ever supplied to North America, most of them in 1949. Sales, in any case, started very slowly, for only 43 cars were completed in 1948. 586 followed in 1949, but demand was already beginning to ebb away, and the last of all these models was built in the autumn of 1950.

Of the 877 produced, only 251 had left-hand steering, for most right hand drive export cars went to what we now rather quaintly call the 'British Empire Countries', notably to Australia and South Africa.

(Left) Although all YTs went to 'export' customers., many of them had Right Hand steering.
(Right) The YT was a four-seater, but only had two passenger doors. These hinged at the rear – an arrangement which would later become unfashionable.

This was the chassis plate of the YT Tourer, giving every chassis detail of the car.

The style of the post-war YT was a throwback to the 1930s, for the doors had a cutaway shape, and detachable side-screens.

The trunk lid of the YT folded down, but the straps were strong enough to support considerable loads.

SPECIFICATIONS

Production: 877

Body styles: Four-seater open tourer

Construction: Steel chassis, wood and steel body

Engine: Four-cylinders, 1,250cc.

Power Output: 54bhp

Transmission: Four-speed manual

Suspension: Front – independent, coil springs, rear - beam axle, leaf springs

Brakes: Front drums, rear drums

Maximum speed: 76 mph (122km/h)

0-60mph (0-96 km/h): 27.0sec

1949-53 *TD Midget*

Four years after Abingdon had started making sports car again, MG was ready to produce a new model. Although the TC was replaced by the TD in January 1950, the new model was much more than a mere replacement for the old. By MG's previous sports car standards, there was a revolution in the design of its chassis.

Except for its style, which still featured free standing headlamps, running boards at each side of the cockpit, a fold-flat windscreen, and very basic all-weather equipment, the TD was the first post-war MG sports car to have what was then considered a modern chassis. Not only did it have a much softer ride than that of the TC, but it also had independent front suspension, rack-and-pinion steering and a box-section chassis frame.

Compared with the TC, the technical difference was complete. Whereas the TC had merely been the latest in an MG pedigree which

had effectively been established with the M-Type of 1928, the TD was not related to those cars at all. The TC, and all earlier Midgets, had a narrow-based and rather flexible chassis frame, with very hard leaf spring suspension, and with beam axles at both ends. The TD though looking very similar to the casual onlooker, had a much sturdier, box-section, frame, and coil spring front suspension.

Below: *The TD was the very first road-going MG sports car to have independent front suspension. It was a big hit in North America.*

The TD's running gear, in fact, had evolved directly from that of the YA sedan, which had been on sale since 1947. Although the chassis side rails were re-aligned to sweep up and over the top of the rear axle line, and the wheelbase was shortened by five inches, the general layout, and the complete front suspension/steering installation were retained. The same 54bhp/1,250cc engine, and its related four-speed transmission were retained – which meant that there had now been no improvement in T-Series power output since 1939.

At the same time this meant that bolt-on steel disc wheels had to be used, which was another 'first' for an MG sports car (such wheels had also been used in the YA sedan, but on no other previous MG), and provision was finally made for left-hand steering to be fitted. This was a vital advance, for it meant that sales to North America might (and in fact did) boom ahead.

To complete this amalgam – and it was certainly a rather rushed job which was conceived at Abingdon, rather than at Cowley, where design leadership remained – MG elected to up-date, rather than completely change, the general style of the T-Series sports car. Compared with the TC, the new car which we would come to know as the TD had the same wheelbase but wider tracks (five whole inches wider at the rear), and used 15in. wheels with fatter tires instead of 19in. wheels with very skinny treads.

All in all, this made the TD a much squatter, somehow more purposeful, car than the TC had ever been, and the lines of the two-seater tourer body were re-vamped to suit. Here was a body which looked wide enough (may I be excused for saying 'for the first time'), and there was just the important bit of extra space in and around the engine to help all enthusiastic owners find space to service, or to tinker. Even so, some MG traditions, like the exposed headlamps, and the big, exposed, 'slab' fuel tank, were retained.

This all made a big difference to the attitude of the car, to its stance, to its presence on the road. The TD, somehow, looked as if might corner much harder, and provide more creature comforts, than the TC had ever done. This, in fact, is precisely what was delivered. In the UK the first TD's cost £569, in the USA $2,115. No rival in the same class could match this price, so all over the world sales took off like a rocket.

In particular, North American customers loved the fact that they could now have left-hand steering. Maybe they were not too enamoured of the rather plain-Jane looks (though a change from plain to perforated wheels helped), but they loved the inch-accurate steering, the pliant ride, and the fact that the engine could

MILESTONE FACTS

- The TD was the first-ever MG sports car to use independent front suspension.
- The TD was the first MG sports car to be built with a choice of right-hand and left-hand steering
- More TDs were built than the entire pre-war output of Abingdon in the 1920s and 1930s
- The TD's chassis design evolved from that of the YA saloon, but with the side members swept up and over the rear axle, another MG 'first'.
- The TD was the first MG sports car to use rack-and-pinion steering
- The TD was the first MG sports car to use steel disc wheels

be power-tuned if they wanted to do this.

Once the word got around, MG found itself taking an unprecedented number of TD orders, which not only filled Abingdon to its limits, but it also taxed the Morris Bodies factory in Coventry, who had never before had to build so many wood/steel structures in any one time. MG's total output rose from 7,046 cars in 1949, to 10,430 in 1950, and to 11,065 in 1951. No fewer than 7,451 Tds were built in 1951 – of which 5,757 went to the USA.

Development changes eventually led to the TD becoming known (internally, but never on the advertising hoardings !) as the 'TDII', but this model must never be confused with a sub-derivative, the TD Mk II. These machines were intended for competition use, and were built to special order, in small numbers, with a variety of specifications. Engines could have up to 61bhp, some cars had revised axle ratios, and some had extra Andrex friction-type dampers fitted at front and rear.

Once thought to be extremely rare, we now know that 1,710 such Mk Iis were produced, of which no fewer than 1,593 examples were sold in the USA. Not only that, but MG also developed a series of engine 'Stage' tune-up kits, the most powerful of which developed nearly 70bhp at more than 6,000rpm.

Demand for TDs held up remarkably well, for no fewer than 10,838 cars were produced in 1952, and at times more than 1,000 cars were being assembled every month at Abingdon. This car, however, reached the end of its run in August 1953, when it was replaced by the TF, which was really no more than a facelift of the original TD.

(Far Left) Free-standing headlamps were definitely 'retro' by 1949 – but the TD had them.
(Left) The TD's engine bay was crowded, even though the 1,250cc engine is a very compact unit.

(Above) The headlamps of the TD were supported on rails connecting the front wings to the radiator shell.

TWL 577

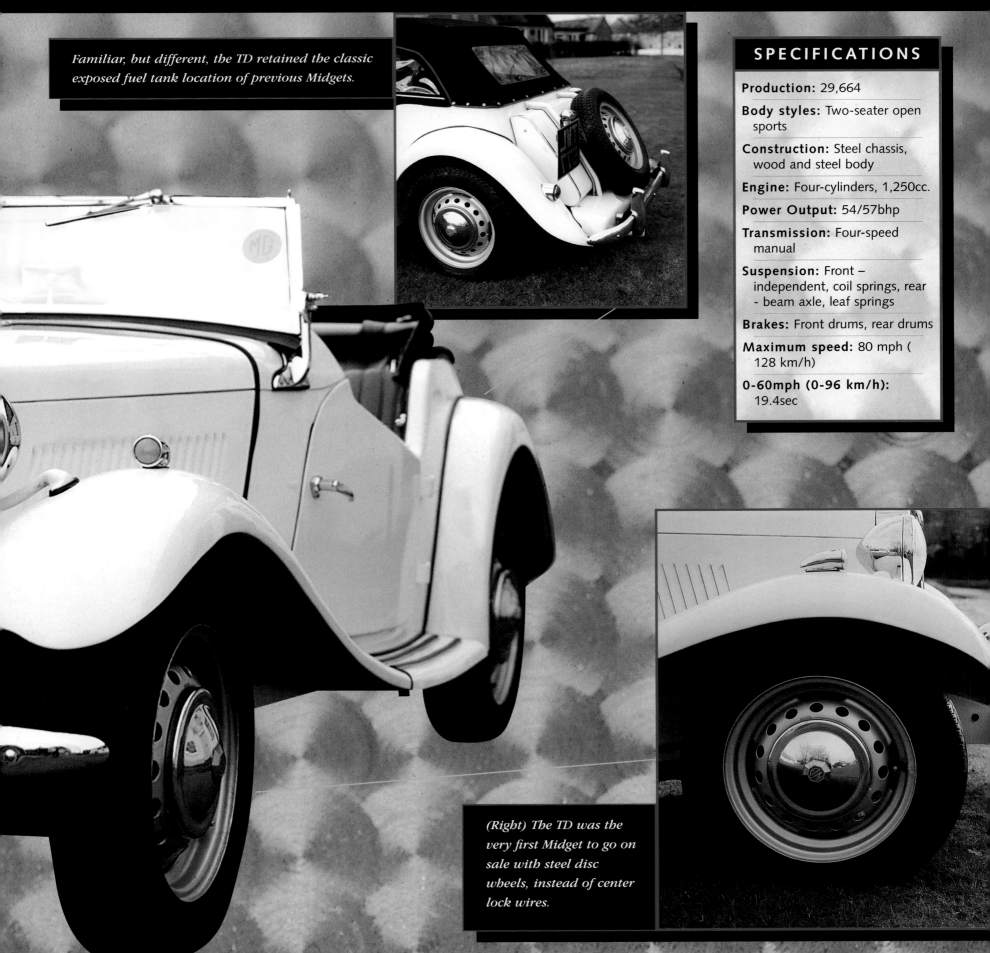

Familiar, but different, the TD retained the classic exposed fuel tank location of previous Midgets.

SPECIFICATIONS

Production: 29,664

Body styles: Two-seater open sports

Construction: Steel chassis, wood and steel body

Engine: Four-cylinders, 1,250cc.

Power Output: 54/57bhp

Transmission: Four-speed manual

Suspension: Front – independent, coil springs, rear - beam axle, leaf springs

Brakes: Front drums, rear drums

Maximum speed: 80 mph (128 km/h)

0-60mph (0-96 km/h): 19.4sec

(Right) The TD was the very first Midget to go on sale with steel disc wheels, instead of center lock wires.

1953-55 *TF Midget*

Although many MG enthusiasts still believe that the TF was the prettiest of all the traditional-style MG sports cars, the fact is that development was something of a rush job, and sales were not as high as the planners had ever hoped. The TF, in fact, was evolved because more ambitious plans to develop a more advanced two-seater (which would become the MGA) were put on 'hold' by the new top management at BMC.

After the 1952 London Motor Show, where two smart two-seater prototypes – of the Austin-Healey 100 and the Triumph TR2 - had been shown, morale at MG took a dive. Suddenly the existing TD not only looked old fashioned, but was about to be outranked in performance too. Because both the rivals could be in production by the summer of 1953, MG needed to do something – anything – to match that enterprise.

With little time to spare, and virtually no development funds available, MG mocked up what they thought could be done to facelift the TD, and showed it to their new bosses in January 1953. Approval came at once, but it took until October 1953 before the new derivative, titled TF, was ready for sale.

The basis of the TF was the TDII, for it retained the same chassis, the same basic running gear, and the same basic body shell, but

Below: *The TF was the last of the traditionally-styled Midgets. Its centre section was that of the TD, but the front end had been lowered, and smoothed out.*

with a considerable facelift at front and rear. Miraculously, MG's own staff – no stylists, nothing as advanced as that, merely resourceful managers and development engineers – had evolved a new frontal aspect, new flowing wings along the flanks, and a much-revised tail.

At the front, this was to be the very first MG to have a sloping-back version of the famous radiator grille, and it was also the first to have headlamps faired in to the sexily flared front wing/valance pressings. The radiator shell itself was lower, which meant that the hood panels sloped down significantly towards the nose. At the rear the big fuel tank was raked back at its base, and the rear wings were flared to suit.

The TF, too, would have wire-spoke wheels as an option to steel disc wheels, which made all the difference to the style and character. Wires had never been available on the TD (very late on in the TD's life, in theory, a kit could be bought, but I have never seen such a car), this being an omission for which many die-hard MG enthusiasts never forgave the company.

Inside the cockpit there was a new instrument display, where the octagon styled instruments were grouped into a central panel display, with open cubby boxes positioned on each side. Even on this car, by the way, MG still did not offer a fuel contents gauge – that would have to wait for the MGA of 1955.

The overall result was that the TF was a car which looked less angular, less severe, and somehow looked smaller than the TD which it replaced. This was pure visual illusion, of course, for the wheelbase and track dimensions were the same as before.

Under the skin, the mechanical changes were very limited. The well-known 1,250cc engine was power-tuned slightly, and was now to be rated at 57bhjp, instead of 54bhp. This figure was still only slightly higher than it had originally been in the TB of 1939 – those changes being due to the fitment of larger SU carburetors, and to the tiny pancake air cleaners which were needed to squeeze the engine into the slimmed-down body panels.

Incidentally, this was also the first MG sports car to be sold with an 'MG radiator' which was a sham – for on this, and on all subsequent, MG sports cars, the radiator itself was a separate block, hidden immediately behind the bright-work.

MILESTONE FACTS

- The TF 1500 was the only MG sports car to use the 1,466cc version of the famous T-Series four-cylinder engine
- The TF was the first MG to use a sloping-back radiator grille style, and the first to feature semi-recessed headlamps.
- On the TF model, MG once again made centre-lock wire wheels and option.
- The TF model was a hastily conceived stopgap product – engineered and styled first, with the drawings following months later.
- The TF was the very last MG production car to feature a body shell built up of steel panels on a wooden framework.

The TF went on sale in the UK, priced at £780, which was slightly more than the £752 asked for the last of the TDs, and that price had been set very keenly to match that of Triumph's new TR2, which was a 105mph car priced at £787. Although its initial reception was warm, there was no doubt that the market place had expected more of a successor to the TD, so sales rather dragged during the winter of 1953/1954. Abingdon settled down to building about 200 TFs every week, most of which would be delivered in North America.

The North American dealers, however, could not sell the TF at the same rate as the TD, so requests for more power, or other improvements, soon started to flow back into Abingdon. Road & Track, which was the sports car buyer's bible in those days, had called it 'an anomaly – a retrogression', and the clientele did not like that.

Accordingly, as a last attempt to keep the TF competitive until the new MGA could be brought in during 1955, from July 1954 it was upgraded to the TF1500, with an enlarged and much re-worked version of the famous XP-series engine. Now of 1,466cc, with an enlarged cylinder bore, it produced 63bhp instead of 57bhp, and helped to push up the top speed of the car to at least 85mph, and to carve a couple of seconds off the 0-60mph sprint.

Almost all of these cars were delivered to the USA (the TF1500, officially, was never launched at all in the UK), and in fact no fewer than 3,400 TF1500s (of the total TF sanction of 9,600) were produced before TF assembly finally ran out in April 1955.

When the TF was discontinued, it brought to an end the era of the traditionally styled MG sports car, for the MGA which replaced it was different in all respects.

Although the octagon motif looked familiar, everything else about the TF's dashboard was new, with centrally-mounted instruments.

(Above) Tightly-packed engine bay (Below) The headlamp guards were a personal accessory on this TF.

OXJ 5

The TF could be bought with wire wheels or steel discs – most buyers chose wires.

SPECIFICATIONS

Production: 9,600 (of which 3,400 were TF1500s)

Body styles: Two-seater open sports

Construction: Steel chassis, wood and steel body

Engine: Four-cylinders, 1,250/1,466cc.

Power Output: 57/63bhp

Transmission: Four-speed manual

Suspension: Front – independent, coil springs, rear - beam axle, leaf springs

Brakes: Front drums, rear drums

Maximum speed: 80 mph (128 km/h)/85mph (137 km/h)

0-60mph (0-96 km/h): 18.9sec/16.3sec

(Left) Wing mirrors – another period option on this TF.

(Below) Wire spoke wheels on the TF – nice to be back, for they were not available on the TD.

81

1953-58 ZA & ZB Magnette

Plans to replace the Y-Type sedan had originally been laid in 1949, but little was achieved until Gerald Palmer took over at Cowley, as the new MG/Riley/Wolseley sedan car design chief, in 1949. Starting at once, but with many pauses, changes of corporate direction, and finally the merger of Nuffield with Austin along the way, Palmer eventually conceived a new car, which became known as the ZA Magnette.

Here was a car influenced by the latest, sleek, Italianate styling trends, which would break all existing records for the sale of MG sedans. Indeed, until the arrival of the MGA sports car, it would be the best-selling MG of all time. By 1950s standards it was a great MG in every way, for it looked good, handled extremely well, and was a much faster car than the sweet, but rather pedestrian, YB which it would replace.

Designed in parallel with the Wolseley 4/44 model, and sharing the same basic body structure and suspension layouts, it was the very first unit-construction (monocoque) MG to be put on sale.

The body shell, in fact, was always pressed and assembled by Pressed Steel, at Cowley (this factory was, literally, across the road from Morris) – this being yet another 'first' for MG, who had previously patronised other body manufacturers. Oddly enough, the Wolseley used a de-tuned version of the Y-Type's 1,250cc engine, and related gearbox, whereas the Z-Type Magnette was always fitted with the new, corporate, BMC B-Series engine.

Below: *The ZA Magnette, introduced in 1953, was a sleekly styled sedan, influenced by the latest fashions from Italy.*

This, in itself, was no bad thing, for it proved to be a remarkably robust and tuneable power unit. In one form or another the B-Series would come to be fitted to a myriad of Austin, Morris, MG, Riley and Wolseley cars of the 1950 – 1970s period, including the MGBs which raced at Le Mans in the 1960s. In fact the ZA Magnette was the very first British Motor Corporation car to have the B-Series fitted, and in initial guise it developed 60bhp. This was enough to guarantee 80mph, which made the new Magnette equally as rapid as the TF with which it originally shared space at Abingdon.

Suspension and steering, hidden away under the sleek new skin, was conventional. At the front there was independent suspension, by coil springs and wishbones, with rack-and-pinion steering, while there was a hypoid bevel beam axle at the rear. In a sure sign that BMC rationalisation was setting in very rapidly indeed, the Magnette used the new B-Series transmission and rear axle. Original plans to use an axle-locating torque arm at the rear were hastily abandoned when the first production cars were found to handle badly.

Right from the start, the ZA built up a great reputation. Like all MGs of its time, it was really far too sturdily engineered (and, therefore, over-heavy) for the job, which meant that it was neither as fast nor as economical as some might hope. On the other hand, the structure was really rugged, the handling was predictable (with a supple ride), and it seemed to live up to MG's proud slogan of 'Safety Fast'.

The interior, and particularly the fascia, did not quite live up to its original price tag - £915, which put it squarely in the compact/mid-market/sports sedan category – though with leather-faced seats, and with a fascia which might have been metal, but at least looked like wood, there were few real complaints. That price, incidentally, was only £10 more than the last of the YBs, which made the sleek new model look like a real bargain.

It was, in any case, a real sports sedan that felt compact, was crisp and welcoming in its behaviour, made a lot of new owners very happy indeed. Far more than the YA or YB types had ever been, it was clearly suited to export markets too. The first series production cars were produced in February 1954, and nearly 4,000 ZAs

MILESTONE FACTS

- The ZA Magnette was the first MG to use a unit-body/monocoque structure
- The ZA sedan was the first in the entire BMC group to use the new B-Series engine
- The ZA Magnette revived a famous early-1930s name, which had previously been applied to sports cars.
- ZA Magnettes were used in the 'works' motorsport team in the mid/late 1950s.
- The ZA was the first MG to have a body shell supplied by Pressed Steel, of Cowley
- With total sales of 36,601, the Z-Series Magnette set new all-time sales records for an MG sedan model

would be produced in that calendar year. Then production – and sales – went ahead with gusto, for no fewer 8,925 would be built in 1955, this being a record, by any measure, for an MG badged sedan.

But there was more to come. From the autumn of 1956 MG upgraded this well-liked car, making visual and technical changes, and dubbing it ZB. Although it does not always apply, in this case second thoughts were definitely better thoughts. The customers clearly thought so, for even more ZBs than ZAs were sold, in a shorter time.

Visually, the changes were mainly cosmetic, for there were changes to the fascia, instruments and steering wheel designs, but in addition a sub-type called the 'Varitone' was also made available. Not only was this available with two-tone paint-work, but it was also fitted with a larger rear window. A more powerful engine (68bhp instead of 60bhp) was fitted to all ZBs, this engine actually being fitted to the last of the ZAs too. A clutchless gearchange (Manumatic) was also made available – the 'clutch' was actuated whenever the driver handled the gear shift itself – though this was not at all popular, with only 496 such cars being produced.

The Z-Series Magnettes remained popular throughout their five year life, and naturally set new sales records at Abingdon for a sedan model. It tells us everything that the highest sales were achieved in the final full year – 1958, when 9,438 cars (nearly 200 such cars every working week) had to be built at Abingdon to meet the demand.

The changeover, from Z-Series built at Abingdon, to the new Mk III, which was produced at BMC's Cowley factory, was dramatic and salutary.

Very neat instrument binnacle on the ZA Magnette, though perhaps the wheel was a bit too large.

The body was engineered so that the grille of the ZA lifted up when the hood was raised.

Coil spring independent suspension, allied to rack-and-pinion steering, was a feature of the ZA Magnette.

(Left) The clock was mounted on the windshield header rail, a very neat touch.

(Right) The MG octagon on the trunk lid told its own story, for the word 'Magnette' was never spelt out.

SPECIFICATIONS

Production: 18,076/18,525

Body styles: Four-door sedan

Construction: Steel unit-construction body/chassis

Engine: Four-cylinders, 1,489cc.

Power Output: 60bhp/68bhp

Transmission: Four-speed manual

Suspension: Front – independent, coil springs, rear - beam axle, leaf springs

Brakes: Front drums, rear drums

Maximum speed: 80 mph (128 km/h)

0-60mph (0-96 km/h): 22.6sec

1958-62 *MGA 1600*

In 1955 MG caused a sensation. After producing the same basic style of two-seater sports cars for more than 25 years, the company took a giant leap into modernity. To follow up the traditional-looking TF, MG revealed the MGA, which was different – and more modern – in every respect. MG enthusiasts loved what they were offered.

Not only would the MGA sell in record numbers, but it would be the mainstay of Abingdon's business for the next seven years. Even as early as 1952, MG had wanted to replace the TD with a modern new car, which they coded EX175, but this project was cancelled by the new BMC management. The TF followed on, instead. It was not until 1954 that an up-dated version of this car, coded EX182, was finally approved. This signalled the re-opening of an engineering design at Abingdon, where Syd Enever took control of new projects.

EX182 – which would soon be officially named MGA – was almost totally different from the T-Series cars which it replaced. Not only did it have a new chassis, and smart new body styling, but it

Above: *Before putting the MGA on sale, MG raced a trio of light-alloy-bodied cars at the Le Mans 24 Hour race in June 1955.*
Above right: *In seven years, well over 100,000 MGAs of all types were manufactured. This was Car. Number 100,000 being finished off in 1962.*
Opposite page: *The 50,000th MGA was produced in 1959. Alongside it, in this picture, is an Austin-Healey Sprite 'bug eye'.*

also used a corporate BMC engine and transmission. The only carryover engineering (and even that was modified in detail) was the coil spring independent front suspension and rack-and-pinion steering as seen in TD/TF/YA/YB models.

The chassis frame was massively strong, with box section side members and a sturdy steel structure under the scuttle/bulkhead area. The engine itself was a much-modified BMC B-Series unit of 1,489cc (as already in use in the ZA Magnette), and was backed by the same four-speed gearbox and hypoid back axle units.

The body style, though, was the star, for it was a smart, gently curving, two-seater in which a full-width cockpit and flowing front wings did away completely with running boards. The MGA grille was still there, but no longer in what we may call 'radiator shape' – for the first time it lay well back into the streamlined bodywork which also had no external door/trunk handles, made this a design classic instantly. Inside the car, most octagon insignia had disappeared, for here was a car with a simple fascia, and circular Jaeger instruments.

Not only was this a visually attractive style – and one which would not 'date' in the next seven years – but it was the most aerodynamically-efficient MG road car yet produced. At a stroke, therefore, the car's top speed was pushed up to the high 'nineties – and MGs were performance competitive once again.

Aluminum-bodied prototypes raced at Le Mans in June 1955, but all production cars had a steel shell with aluminum doors, hood and trunk lid, and a bubble-top coupe version, with wind-up windows, came along a year later. The MGA was so successful that it broke every MG sales record. By the time the original MGA1500 was up-graded, to MGA1600, in mid-1959, no fewer than 58,750 had been produced.

The MGA1600 not only received an 80bhp/1,588cc version of the engine, but was fitted with front-wheel disc brakes as standard, and was a genuine 100mph car, the first-ever MG road car to achieve that magic figure. Although it was not as powerful as the twin-Cam model (which is described on pages 90-93), it was an excellent all-round package, whose performance was matched by its handling, and sheer practicality. It was no wonder that this was a highly-prized and seductive offering. The American buyers, in particular, loved the car – though far more Roadsters than Coupes were eventually produced – for here was a truly fast MG which also offered a cockpit which was finally wide-enough, and comfortable enough, for two full-sized adults. Not only that, but the MGA was the first two-seater MG sports car which had a separate and enclosed trunk. Since it was no longer considered decadent to want to be warm, and to know what was happening in the wide world. A heater and a radio could both be added as optional extras.

The MGA1600 was even more popular with the clientele that the MGA1500 had ever been, so no fewer than 31,501 were sold in two years. Even though MG assembly at Abingdon was being squeezed by the arrival of the new Austin-Healey 'bug eye' Sprite on a parallel assembly line, this was still yet another record rate for the MG marque.

At this time, too, there was a little-known model known as the 1600 De Luxe, which was effectively an amalgam of Twin-Cam chassis (four-wheel disc brakes and all) together with the existing 1.6-liter overhead-valve engine, a car which would be produced until 1962, when MGA assembly finally ended.

The final derivative of this much-loved design – more than 100,000 of all MGA types would eventually be built – was the MGA1600 Mk II, which appeared in mid-1961. Based strongly on the 1600, it featured an engine which had been enlarged very slightly – from 1,588cc to 1,622cc – where the peak power went up

MILESTONE FACTS

- The MGA used a body style originally developed for use at the Le Mans 24 Hour race.

- The MGA 1600 was the very first MG with an independently recorded top speed of more than 100mph

- The MGA was the first 'modern style' MG sports car and the first to use an all-steel body shell.

- The MGA was the first-ever MG to be available with a steel bubble-top hardtop.

- Front-wheel disc brakes were fitted to the MGA, the 1600, from 1959. This was a 'first' for MG.

- In seven years, three types of B-Series engined MGAs were produced.

- More than 100,000 MGAs were produced, this being a new record for any MG model.

from 80bhp (1600) to 93bhp (1600 Mk II). Because of this, and the fatter torque curve, this allowed the rear axle ratio to be raised, and converted the MGA into an even more satisfying freeway cruiser. Visually the only significant changes were the arrival of a modified front grille, and yet another type of rear lamp cluster.

Only 8,719 Mk IIs of all types were ever produced, for assembly finally halted in the summer of 1962, This was done, not because the MGA had stopped selling, but because extensive preparations were needed to start building Abingdon's all-time best-seller, the MGB.

(Below) Every line of the MGA style was neatly integrated. The driving lamp on this car was an owner's accessory fitment.

(Above) A full display of controls and dials on the MGA.
(Left) Like many proud owners, this MGA custodian has chosen to add streamlined wing mirrors.

SPECIFICATIONS

Production: 31,501/8,719

Body styles: Two-seater open sports/coupe

Construction: Steel chassis, and body shell. Aluminum panels.

Engine: Four-cylinders, 1,588cc/1,622cc.

Power Output: Standard 80bhp/93bhp car featured 115bhp

Transmission: Four-speed manual

Suspension: Front - independent, coil springs, rear beam axle, leaf springs

Brakes: Front discs, rear drums

Maximum speed: 101 mph car featured 115mph (162km/h)

0-60mph (0-96 km/h): 14.2sec car featured 8.8 secs.

(Left) On the hardtop version of the MGA 1600, the door handles were neatly arranged in a vertical layout.
(Below) This rally plate reminds everyone that this particular car competed in the snows of Monte Carlo.

(Above) Function and flair – standard tail lamps, snap-action filler cap (an accessory fitment) and extra reversing lamps, all give this particular car a flair.

1958-61 MGA Twin Cam

Because MG could never operate independently of its financial masters, it's engineers rarely got approval to produce something ultra-fast, exotic, or expensive. Occasionally, just occasionally, an exception was made.

Even so, in the 1950s it was a surprise to hear that BMC had allowed not one, but two, twin-overhead-camshaft engines to be designed – and it was an even bigger surprise when one of them went into production in 1958 for a car called the MGA Twin-Cam.

Way back in 1955, both the 'Austin' and 'Morris' twin-cams were fitted to MGA prototypes ready for the Tourist Trophy race, but problems with the 'Austin' unit saw it abandoned before the race started. The 1,588cc 'Morris' design, which had evolved around the cylinder block of the existing 1600 MGA overhead-valve engine was more successful, went on to power the EX181 record car in 1957, and was the engine chosen for the new MGA Twin-Cam in 1958.

Through no fault of its own, the Twin-Cam would have a short life – announced in July 1958, it was withdrawn in April 1960 – but while it was available it was the fastest and most powerful MG so far put on general sale. With 108bhp from the exquisitely detailed engine, which compared with only 72bhp from the normal MGA's B-Series power unit, it meant that this particular could reach 113mph, and could sprint up to 60mph in less than ten seconds.

Below: Left: *All Twin-Cams were built with special centre-lock Dunlop wheels, as earlier seen on the D-Type Jaguar.*

Coventry, where the engine was designed, was really an overgrown 'motoring village' at the time (just like Detroit, really, but not on the same scale). This explains, therefore, why much of the twin-cam layout and its detailing was like that of the Jaguar XK engine, and the Coventry-Climax FPF race engine, both of which were also produced in the city. It was a bulky, but formidable-looking piece of engineering, which quite filled the engine bay of the existing MGA.

Visually, the Twin-Cam looked similar to the ordinary MGA (although, if you looked closely enough, there were 'Twin Cam' badges close to the engine bay air outlets close to the base of the windshield), though the wheels were of the Dunlop centre-lock disc variety, as already made famous on the Jaguar D-Type. Under those wheels, too, Dunlop disc brakes were fitted to all four wheels. Because of these updates, and because of the bulky nature of the engine, there were significant chassis frame changes too. As an example, to clear the bulkier engine, the steering rack had to be re-positioned one inch further forward, which meant that the rack and the steering arms, had to be specially engineered to suit. At the same time, too, the radiator block was also mounted further forward. This, therefore, was a capable, fast and very balanced derivative of the MGA, and as with the normally-engined types it was available as an open Roadster, or with the alternative bubble-top/wind-up window coupe style.

Visually and functionally the Twin-Cam was a fine car, though it was always seen as expensive to buy, and rather costly to maintain. As launched in the UK, the Twin-Cam Roadster cost £1,266 when the B-Series engined equivalent was priced at only £996. By early twenty-first-century price levels, that £300 gap might sound small, but in 1958 it was actually half the price of a Morris Minor. The Twin-Cam also cost £40 more than the 2.6-liter Austin-Healey 1100-Six, which was being assembled alongside it, at Abingdon.

Twin-Cam assembly started very gently in the summer of 1958 – only 50 cars were produced before the end of August – though things brightened up as soon as more engines were available, so no fewer than 508 had been assembled by the end of the calendar year. Twin-Cam assembly then reached its heights in the spring of 1959 – clearly there was a concerted effort to get ample stocks to North America for the important buying season – with more than 300 cars built in February, and a total of 1,318 produced between January and June 1959. Then, unhappily, production rapidly died away, such that only 232 more cars were produced before the end of the year.

How could this be ? Unhappily, the fact is that the Twin-Cam was already beginning to get a rather difficult reputation in service, with

MILESTONE FACTS

- The MGA Twin-Cam was the very first MG road car to use a twin-overhead-camshaft engine

- The MGA Twin-Cam was the only road car to use this twin-cam engine. It was also used in MG record cars.

- Road wheels of MGA Twin-Cam type had already been used on the Jaguar D-Types which won the Le Mans 24 Hour race three times.

- The MGA Twin-Cam had four-wheel disc brakes. This was a world 'first' for road cars. This was the first time disc brakes were used on an MG road car.

- The MGA 1600 De Luxe which followed was really a Twin-Cam, but with a different, overhead-valve, engine

quite a few engines suffering from burnt pistons, most of them suffering from excessive oil consumption – and almost all of them giving headaches to mechanics in dealerships who had never had to deal with such a complex engine before.

MG had already picked up these vibrations, and made significant changes which quite transformed the engine before the end of its life. Reputations, however, are usually lost much faster than they can be re-built, and out in the market place the damage was done. Only 53 cars were built in 1960 before MG pulled the plug.

As with the Triumph Stag, for instance, surviving MGA Twin-Cams are all well-loved, all with rock-solid reliable engines, and all are much-prized classics. At the time, though, MG was happy to pull back from such a costly programme, and would never again produce such a specialized road car.

There was, however, and interesting sequel. Soon after the Twin-Cam was abandoned, MG knew that they would have to something to clear the stocks of Twin-Cam rolling chassis which had already been produced. This led to the appearance of a car named the MGA 1600 de Luxe, a type which, although little advertised, remained on sale until the summer of 1962.

Although the specification of the de Luxes varied significantly between individual cars, effectively these were Twin Cams which had been fitted with the more mundane B-series engine, either of 1,588cc or (from 1961) of 1,622cc. MG's own chassis records, which have been preserved, show that no fewer than 395 such cars were built, of which 82 had the earlier, 1,588cc, engine. Only 35 of all these cars were Coupes, just 12 of them having 1,588cc engines.

(Below) The MGA had a small boot stowage area, in which the spare wheel took up most of the space.

Above) There were three different tail lamp designs in the seven-year life of the MGA. This is the early type.

(Left) All MGAs had twin air outlets ahead of the windshield, which channeled hot air out of the engine bay. *(Below)* The Twin-Cam engine itself was bulky, and filled up the MGA's engine bay, with not much space left for servicing.

SPECIFICATIONS

Production: 2,111 Coupe and Roadster

Body styles: Two-seater Coupe, and Roadster

Construction: Steel chassis, steel body

Engine: Four-cylinders, 1,588cc.

Power Output: 108bhp

Transmission: Four-speed manual

Suspension: Front – independent, coil springs, rear - beam axle, leaf springs

Brakes: Front discs, rear discs

Maximum speed: 113 mph (182 km/h)

0-60mph (0-96 km/h): 9.1sec

(Below) Dunlop knock-on disc wheels were a feature of the twin-Cam, and the closely-related 1600 De Luxe model.

1959-68 *Magnette* Mk III & MK IV

By the late 1950s MG had once again lost much of its independence, for it was a constituent of the BMC empire, and had to fall in with the product plans being developed at HQ, at Longbridge, near Birmingham. When the elegant ZA/ZB Magnette sedan came to the end of its life in 1958, BMC decided to replace it with a new Austin-based car.

The MG business at Abingdon had nothing to do with the evolution of the new car, which was entirely designed at Longbridge, and would be assembled at the Nuffield factory at Cowley, near Oxford.

The new car, called Magnette Mk III, was everything that the ZB had never been. Although it retained the same basic B-Series engine, transmission and rear axle as the ZB had used (BMC rationalisation policy was well advanced), it had a totally different body shell, structure and front suspension layout. For a new range of cars, BMC had retained the styling services of the famous Italian styling house, Farina, and had elected to make five different versions of this new style, which would carry Austin, Morris, Riley, Wolseley and MG badges. The public would be able to pick up the differences became of the individual front-end styles, and there would be significant gradations of engine power, paint jobs, furnishing, and overall equipment.

When consulted, Farina offered a new squared-up theme which was very much in line with modern European trends. For BMC, not only did this produce a more spacious cabin, but there was to be a much larger trunk, and rather obvious rear fins. In the MG version

there would be a wooden fascia, and wood cappings on the door, along with a variety of MG and (semi-) octagon motifs on the instrument panel.

Compared with the well-loved ZB, the difference was enormous, for the ZB had been curvaceous, looked smaller than it actually was, and could be turned into a competent, if over-heavy, competition sedan. The Mk III, on the other, actually seemed to be slightly larger than it actually was, certainly did not handle as well (though the ride was softer), and offered nothing much to sporty-minded drivers.

MG's bosses at BMC knew this, and didn't care. Economically it made sense to mix-and-match bodies and badges in this manner (they had been taking lessons from GM, who had much more experience with the same process), and as long as the marketing message was clear, they were sure that sales would follow. To get the Mk III off to a flying start, they set its price at exactly that of the out-going ZB - £1,072 in the UK.

Although sales never quite matched what had been achieved at Abingdon, they were encouraging enough. At its peak, 9,438 ZBs had been produced in a single year, while 7,812 Mk IIIs were produced in 1959, and another 7,145 followed in 1960. The new car was quick enough – 84 – 85mph was attainable – but the car, somehow, lacked the sporting character of the old ZB, and seemed to sell to a different clientele. Even though the engine was almost as powerful as that of the MGA, there was less urgency than the old ZB had shown – and there is no doubt that the ride and handling was not nearly as good.

BMC, to their credit, reacted quite briskly to this, and introduced a better car, the Magnette Mk IV, in the autumn of 1961. Along with all the cars in this range, without altering the basic body shell, or tampering with the styling, the wheel tracks were pushed out by two inches, and the wheelbase by two inches. At the same time,

Left: *The Magnette Mk III of 1959 was styled by Pininfarina, and built at Cowley.*

MILESTONE FACTS

- The Magnette Mk III was the first-ever post-war MG road car to be assembled away from Abingdon – at the BMC (Morris) factory at Cowley.

- The Magnette Mk III featured styling by the Italian specialist, Pinin Farina

- The Magnette Mk III was one of five-closely-related cars of the same type, most of which were badged 'Austin' or 'Morris'

- Automatic transmission became optional on the Magnette Mk IV – this was the first time anyone could buy an 'automatic' MG.

- The engine of the Magnette Mk IV was almost identical to that being fitted to the MGA 1600 Mk II.

an anti-sway bar was added to the front suspension, and the ride height was lowered – the overall result being a car which looked more purposeful and certainly handled better than before.

Mechanically the big change was that the engine had been enlarged, to 1,622cc (the same size, incidentally, as the MGA 1600 Mk II, which was currently in production at Abingdon), and for the very first time on an MG there was to be the option of automatic transmission. This was the British-built Borg Warner Type 35, a three-speed design especially developed with small-engined cars in mind, and was also to be offered on other cars in this BMC range.

Although the Mk IV was a definite step forward (and was significantly faster than the Mk III), it was a model which BMC – and MG for that matter – thereafter seemed to ignore. For the next six years, no less, the Mk IV carried on with little attention from the publicity gurus, and with no styling or mechanical novelties to rise its profile. Although 3,299 cars were sold in its full year – 1962 – this figure dropped to 2,116 in 1965, and dropped thereafter.

There seemed to be very little interest in automatic transmission cars – 1,699 such were built – and although exports to the USA had been strong in the early years they virtually disappeared after 1962. Along with the other 'B-series Farinas' (as they were always known in the trade, and by industry insiders), the car then jogged on, even while many new-type front-wheel-drive models (including the MG1100/MG1300 types) flourished around it. Only 688 were produced in 1967, and after the formation of British Leyland was announced in January 1968, the very last of these Magnettes were produced. They would not be replaced, and a once-famous model name died out.

(Left) One feature of the squared-up Magnette Mk III was the sizeable trunk space.

(Below) This was how BMC badged the Mk III. There were four other, differently-badged, versions of this body shell.

(Left) Neat and integrated tail lamp clusters on the Mk III.

BMC added a touch of glamour to the Mk III with a wood fascia and well-equipped instrument board.

Plenty of space in the engine bay for the B-Series engine, which was very similar to that of the MGA sports car.

SPECIFICATIONS

Model: Mk II/Mk IV Magnette

Production: 16,648/14,356

Body styles: Four-door sedan

Construction: Steel unit-construction body/chassis

Engine: Four-cylinders, 1,489cc/1,622cc.

Power Output: 66bhp/68bhp

Transmission: Four-speed manual/optional automatic

Suspension: Front – independent, coil springs rear - beam axle, leaf springs

Brakes: Front drums, rear drums

Maximum speed: 84 mph (135 km/h)/86 mph (138 km/h)

0-60mph (0-96 km/h): 20.6sec/19.5sec

1961-79 *Midget*

When that famous MG model name of 'Midget' was revived in 1961 (it had last been seen in 1955), there was rejoicing – until, that is, the origins of the new model sank in. Because BMC was now deeply into the rationalisation process which such a business needed, it had decided that the Midget could not be a new model on its own – but would have to be closely based on the Austin-Healey Sprite.

New readers start here. To build on the success of larger-engined Austin-Healeys, BMC decided to produce a new small sports car. Using a brand new monocoque body/chassis unit (the first, therefore, to appear behind an MG badge), this car was designed by the Healey engineering team, and picked up modified versions of existing Morris Minor 1000 and Austin A35 running gear and suspensions. The engine was the latest version of the ubiquitous little overhead valve A-Series four-cylinder power unit, which had been introduced in 1951, and which would eventually have a corporate life of nearly half-a-century.

The Austin-Healey Sprite, which was always assembled at the MG factory at Abingdon, went on sale in 1958, when it had a particularly odd-looking front end which featured what are often called 'bug-eye' headlamps, and no exterior access to the boot area. This soon gained a reputation as an eager, agile, if not very fast little sports car.

When the time came for a face-lift, the powers-that-be decided that the same car should be made behind two badges – Austin-Healey and MG. According, from 1961 to 1971 (when the Austin-

Below: *Midgets were built for 18 years, with many minor facelifts. This was a late 1960s/early 1970s 1,275cc engined example.*

Healey Sprite identity was finally laid to rest) the two cars co-existed, side-by-side, after which the Midget carried on until the end of 1979.

Compared with the original 'bug eye', the new Sprite Mk II/Midget had a more conventional front body style (in fact it looked rather like a more severe, if smaller, version of the MGB which would shortly follow), though it retained the cantilever quarter-elliptic spring rear suspension of that car. Sports cars in this class were still expected to be rather simply equipped, which explains why the plastic side curtains were removable, and why there was a very simple 'build-it-yourself' soft top to keep out the rain: an optional hardtop was soon made available too.

With the 948cc engine producing 46bhp, it was a cheerful little performer, which could almost reach 90-mph in favourable conditions[downhill]. Not only that, but it was soon clear that the engine could be power-tuned considerably – one result being that 'works' sponsored cars (some of them, I have to admit, carrying Austin-Healey badges) eventually raced with honour in Europe and in North America – and that this could be a great little competition car, at all levels.

For nearly two decades thereafter, the Midget would offer perfect starter-sports-car motoring, in a small and light package. The structure was rock solid, the handling eager, and the running costs low. Although the Midget was considerably smaller than the MGA and MGB, it had a comfortable, compact two-seater cockpit. If and when service and repairs were needed, it was also a simple little car to maintain.

In the next decade, and more, the process of upgrading the Midget went ahead on a regular basis, though the basic style would not be changed until 1974. In every case changes would improve the existing model, either in engine power, in chassis performance, or in equipment. No one ever complained that MG was dabbling without producing a better car. The sales figures, of course, would back this up, for no fewer than 224,839 of these Midgets would eventually be sold – and we should not forget that there were also 129,347 near-identical Sprites

Only 18 months after launch, from late 1962 the Midget was given an enlarged, 55bhp, 1,098cc engine (this being almost identical to the power unit recently fitted to the MG 1100 saloon), and front-wheel disc brakes were standardised at the same time.

Then, in the spring of 1964, the structure was considerably revised. From this point the rear axle was located by conventional half-elliptic leaf springs – this, in fact, altering the balance of the roadholding. These cars were also given a 59bhp engine, and was treated to a body shell having different doors and wind-up

MILESTONE FACTS

- This Midget revived a famous MG model name, which had first been seen 33 years earlier on the M-Type of 1928.
- The Midget of 1961 was closely related to the Austin-Healey Sprite. Both cars were built on the same assembly line.
- Many component parts of the Midget, including the engine and gearbox, were slightly modified versions of those fitted to the Morris Minor family car.
- The Midget was the very first MG sports car to have a unit-body/monocoque structure.
- From 1974 to 1979, the Midget was powered by a Triumph engine. No other MG ever used a Triumph engine.
- Apart from the MGB, the Midget of 1961 – 1979 was the best-selling MG of all time.
- Four different-sized engines were fitted to the Midget in 18 years.

windows, and at the same time a deeper windshield and a more satisfactory folding soft-top mechanism was added. At this point, therefore, the Midget took on the shape and form which would persist for fifteen more years.

Before the end of 1966, the engine was once again boosted – this time to 65bhp and 1,275cc. Although that engine was not quite as specialised as the Mini-Cooper S unit it resembled, it was much more robust that the old 1,098cc engine, and was well liked by the tuners. Then, in 1972, the rear end style was altered a little, with a round rear wheel-arch cut out taking the place of the original squarer style.

The final, and very major, change took place in late 1974. To meet new USA safety legislation, not only was the entire car lifted slightly on its suspension, but vast black polyurethane bumpers were fitted to front and rear. The old BMC unit was ditched, too, in favour of a Triumph Spitfire engine, this not only having 66bhp and 1,493cc, but being better able to meet the exhaust emission rules which were tightening every year in the USA.

Traditionalists did not like the idea of a Triumph engine being fitted, but it prolonged the life of the car (which the A-Series engine could not have done) – and it also made this latter Midget capable of a genuine 100mph. In five years, before assembly at Abingdon eventually ended, 73,899 of this particular model were produced.

The Midget was one of the last two MGs to be built at Abingdon, for the MGB would outlive it by only a further year. After this the factory was closed, sold off, and razed to the ground.

Neat rear corner detailing on the 1960s-style Midget.

(Left) The original Midget of 1961 featured a simple wide-mouth grille. (Right) The early-1960s Midget was a very close-coupled two seater, neatly packaged, but with little stowage space

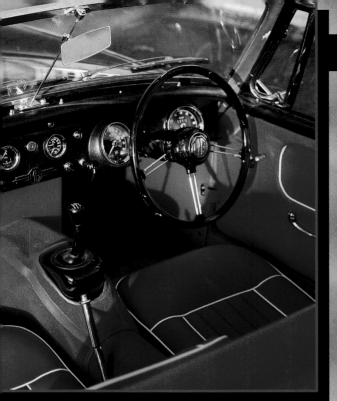

(Below)The 1960s-style Midget used a tuned-up version of the BMC A-Series engine, as used in many of the Group's family cars.

SPECIFICATIONS

Production: 224,839

Body styles: Two-seater open sports

Construction: Steel unit-construction body/chassis

Engine: Four-cylinders, 948cc/1,098cc/1,275cc/1,491 cc.

Power Output: 46bhp/55bhp/59bhp/ 65bhp/65bhp

Transmission: Four-speed manual

Suspension: Front – independent, coil springs, rear - beam axle, leaf springs

Brakes: Front drums (discs from 1962), rear drums

Maximum speed: From 89 mph (km/h) to 101mph (162 km/h)

0-60mph (0-96 km/h): From 16.9sec to 12.3sec

(Above) Center-lock wire-spoke wheels were always optional on the Midget.

1962-67 *MGB* MK I

Although MG first thought about replacing the MGA in the late 1950s, the new model, called MGB, was not ready until the autumn of 1962. There was, after all, no reason to ditch the MGA, for it was selling very well, In any case, Abingdon was far too busy at this time, for introducing the new Midget was a major undertaken which had to be completed first.

In every way the MGB was an obvious, and logical, improvement on the MGA – smoother in style, more powerful, faster, and with a more modern form of construction. As with the Midget, MG took the brave decision to build the MGB around a monocoque structure. Although meant that the capital cost of tooling was higher, it also meant that the new car could be lighter and more rigid.

Although MG's General Manager, John Thornley, knew that he would have to sell more MGBs to make it all worthwhile, he thought this could be done. He was right. The MGB pedigree would persist

Below: *The Morley Twins drove this 'works' MGB to win the GT Category of the 1964 Monte Carlo rally.*

for 18 years, and in the end more than half a million of all types would be built. This was five times as many as the MGA had already achieved. A successful gamble ? You could certainly say that !

Not only did the MGB finally do without a separate chassis frame – this made the MGA the last MG to use such a feature – but it was better packaged than the MGA, with a shorter wheelbase, and a more roomy cockpit. The style had been worked up by MG themselves. Originally, it was said, there were influences from the EX181 'Roaring Raindrop' record car of 1957/1958, but the road car was effectively a larger, more rounded, and extremely attractive up-date of the rather severe style which already existed in the Midget. One slightly controversial feature was the semi-recessed headlamp position, which Renault later complained they had invented for the Floride/Caravelle: MG never reacted, but merely noted that their car was much more successful than the Renault ever was ! It was also the very first mass-produced MG two-seater to be given wind-up windows, though the small Midget would follow suit within 18 months.

Under the skin, the running gear was a logical update as that already found in the MGA. Almost by tradition, the independent front suspension and rack-and-pinion steering gear was carried over from the MGA, this system of course dating back to the YA saloon of 1947. Although MG had originally hoped to use the 1.6-liter engine of the MGA 1600 Mk II, when they saw the need for more performance this was stretched to 1,798cc, a dimension which would then persist for the next 18 years.

Except that the crankshaft was given five main bearings (instead of three) after two years, the specification of this 95bhp power unit was settled throughout the run of the car – and it was enough to give the MGB a top speed of more than 100mph.

Although the four-speed gearbox, with its delightful short-throw change, was the same as before, the MGB was now made available with Laycock overdrive as an option – this being a perfect way of providing higher gearing and more fuel economy. Along with features like the center-lock wire wheels, this would always be a very option: surprisingly, the optional lift-off hardtop was much more rare, even though it was practical and neatly styled.

Once in production, sales and deliveries of the MGB took off like a rocket, especially in North America, where it was successfully marketed. The combination of MG's own brand image, and – by extension – its sheer Britishness, was very attractive to sports car owners, who would keep on returning to this model through a very long and successful life. Successful use in motor racing – specially-modified MGBs, with lengthened noses, competed with honour at

MILESTONE FACTS

- In 18 years, more than half a million MGBs of all types were produced. This made the car the world's highest-selling sports car. It held this title until the 21st Century.

- To finance the costly body press/assembly tooling, MG bartered the capital cost down, but agreed to pay a higher body unit cost.

- Farina had a hand in the styling of the MGB GT

- Early MGBs used 1,798cc engines with three crankshaft bearings: a five-bearing crankshaft was standardised from late 1964.

- Laycock overdrive was optional on the MGB – this being the first time such a fitting was ever offered on an MG .

- When the MGB raced at Le Mans, it was fitted with a long-nose body style. From 1963 to 1965 there were three different cars, but the same nose was handed down from car to car.

Le Mans three times, others were sent to Sebring and the Nurburgring – all added to its do-anything/go-anywhere reputation. The soft ride, the mechanical simplicity, and the sheer hard-working, reliable character all combined to make this the sports car of choice, where rivals from Triumph and Sunbeam struggled hard even to keep abreast.

And this was only the beginning, for the range would soon expand. Three years after the Roadster had gone on sale, MG charmed the marketplace with the very elegant new MGB GT. Not only was this a very practical two-seater fastback coupe, but it also had a lift-up hatchback, a vestigial pair of '+2' seats for tiny children, and was ideal for the many thousands of MG owners who wanted a permanent roof over their heads.

Although MG had conceived the layout at Abingdon, BMC's contracted styling house, Pininfarina of Italy, had smoothed out some of the details. The result was a remarkably pleasing car which was slightly heavier than the Roadster, but otherwise lost nothing to it. No wonder that the buying public liked it so much. In only two years, no fewer than 21,835 MGB GT Mk Is would be built.

Only five years after the MGB had been announced, it was time for change and improvement. Because of the possible cost of changing a unit-body/monocoque shell, there was no question of altering the style, but what became known as the Mk II would be better in all respects. Already the MGB was outselling the much-loved old MGA, and many more records were due to be broken in future.

Left)) This was the original MGB grille style of 1962. It would be altered, in detail, for future models.

(Right) Timeless in its layout, the MGB fascia/instrument layout persisted for many years.

(Below Left) The MGB's boot volume was a great improvement over the MGA, though the spare wheel still had nowhere else to live.

(Below) The MGB's engine was an enlarged, more powerful, version of that used throughout the MGA period.

(Above Left) The original MGB rear-end style of 1962/1963.

SPECIFICATIONS

Production: 137,733 (of which 21,835 were GTs)

Body styles: Two-seater open Roadster, and GT Coupe

Construction: Steel unit-construction body/chassis

Engine: Four-cylinders, 1,798cc.

Power Output: 95bhp

Transmission: Four-speed manual, optional overdrive

Suspension: Front – independent, coil springs, rear - beam axle, leaf springs

Brakes: Front discs, rear drums

Maximum speed: 103 mph (166 km/h)

0-60mph (0-96 km/h): 12.2sec

1962-71 MG 1100/1300 SALOON

In many ways the front-wheel-drive 1100/1300 sedans are the most under-estimated of all MG models. Although they were directly derived from a BMC (Austin-Morris) pedigree, that had many significant technical and equipment differences, and the sort of character that appealed to many drivers of the day. The sales figures back this up – for in ten years no fewer than 143,067 such cars were sold.

After Alec Issigonis's famous Mini was announced in 1959, BMC made haste to adopt the layout for other and larger cars. The Mini had combined a transversely-mounted four-cylinder engine with front-wheel-drive, all-independent suspension, in a small package, and included a cabin which seemed most unfeasibly large for such a small car. The engine itself was an 848cc version of the A-Series power unit which was already slated for use in the MG Midget, and it effectively sat on top of a new four-speed transmission, with which it shared the same lubricant.

Next up, though not announced for three years, was a larger expression of the same theme, and originally meant as a mass-market Austin and Morris model. This new car, mainly engineered by Issigonis's deputy Charles Griffin, was quite a lot larger than the original Mini – it was 147in/3,734mm instead of 120in/3,048mm long – and made much more handsome because it had the latest crisp styling which had been provided by Farina of Italy. The cabin was neatly laid out, much wider and more voluminous than that of the Mini, and was to be made in two-door (export) or four-door (home-market) form.

Although the engine/transmission package was evolved from that of the Mini, the engine itself was now of 1,098cc – very similar indeed to the 1963MY Midget which came along in the same season – while the suspension was by what were called Hydrolastic units. The springs, effectively, were of spheres incorporating rubber casings with water, and were inter-connected front-to-rear. This, boasted BMC, gave the cars a self-levelling effect when passing over rough ground. This was true to an extent, but it also gave them a rather floaty and uneasy feel on smooth roads which some passengers did not enjoy.

As with the 'B-Series Farinas' of 1959 and later, BMC then decided to use GM-style 'badge-engineering' to mould this one new corporate design into several different models. By adding a version of the MG grille up front, by devising a suitably smart fascia style and trim package, and by providing a more powerful twin carburetor (55bhp) version of the engine, this was most credibly achieved, and the MG 1100 began to sell very well. Once assembly

had been properly established at Cowley, no fewer than 26,404 cars were produced in 1963, and even more – 32,703 – followed in 1964.

It really didn't matter what the pundits said, and wrote, for the public definitely loved this car. The handling was good, the steering was accurate and feather light, and the performance was brisk (it was a quicker car than the ageing Magnette Mk IV, which was still being built), all this being delivered in a package with a neatly detailed

Below: *The MG1100/1300 was the marque's first transverse-engined/front-wheel-drive car. This was a facelift 1300 of 1967/1968.*

instrument panel with strip speedo based in a real wood panel.

The fact that this was the-ever front-wheel-drive MG did not seem to harm its prospects at all, especially as it was immediately clear that the chassis, the traction and the general behaviour were of a very high standard. Although this particular version of the A-Series engine was not really suitable for power-tuning, and the structure (like all MGs, it has to be said) was really far too sturdy for the power provided, it was a real sports sedan in all respects.

Like all the models in this BMC range – which also included Austin, Morris, Riley, Vanden Plas and Wolseley-based types - the MG 1100 was extremely successful. More than half the production was exported, which made this car a great earner by any standards.

From 1966/1967, BMC took to altering this range of cars with mind-boggling frequency, and in two years this front-wheel-drive MG changed significantly. Although there were no significant style changes, the engine was progressively improved, moving gradually from 55bhp to no less than 70bhp. In the process the car's top speed jumped from 85mph to 97mph.

MILESTONE FACTS

- The MG 1100 of 1962 was the first-ever MG to have a transverse engine and front wheel drive.

- The MG 1100 had Hydrolastic independent suspension at front and rear. This Moulton-designed system was unique to BMC cars, and fitted to no other MG model.

- The MG 1100 carried a shape by Farina, which was BMC's styling consultant of the period.

- MG 1100s and 1300s were both built with two-door or four-door sedan styles – these being the only MGs ever to have such a choice.

- On the MG 1300, AP automatic transmission became optional – this being the very first time that there had been an automatic transmission MG.

- There were six differently badged versions of this BMC front-wheel-drive saloon. Only the mass-market Austin and Morris types sold faster than the MG.

First along, in spring 1967 was what enthusiasts called the 'MG 1275', for it was really the 1100, fitted with a 1,275cc version of the engine, which had only a single-SU carburetor, but peak power of 58bhp and more torque. As an option to the original, it was only made in small numbers, but from the autumn of 1967 there was also a minor body facelift (the rear fins were cropped, and pierced-type wheels were fitted), which allowed the cars to be called MK 1100 Mk II and MG 1300. The new-type AP four-speed automatic transmission was also made available, but very few such cars were built.

Within six months, everything changed again, for the MG 1100 was dropped, and the MG 1300 was given a more powerful, twin-SU carbureted engine, and 65bhp, but only sold with a two-door, instead of a four-door, body style. The end of the road ? Not by any means, for from October 19698 the MG 1300 officially became MG 1300 Mk II, this time with an even more powerful, 70bhp, version of the engine, and it was this power unit which would power the little MG until it finally ran out in 1971.

In the end, no fewer than 157,409 cars of all types were produced, but at the end of the day there was no successor in sight. Perhaps it could be argued that the very successful Volkswagen Mk 1 Golf effectively evolved around a similar body/engine layout but added a hatch-back which is what this model ultimately lacked..Sadly it would not be until 1982 before a new front-drive MG sports sedan appeared.

SPECIFICATIONS

Model: 1100/1300 saloon

Production: 124,474/32,935

Body styles: Four seater sedan

Construction: Steel unit-construction body/chassis

Engine: Four-cylinders, 1,098cc/1,275cc.

Power Output: 55bhp/60bhp/65bhp/70bhp

Transmission: Four-speed manual, optional automatic

Suspension: Front – independent, Hydrolastic, rear – independent, Hydrolastic

Brakes: Front discs, rear drums

Maximum speed: From 85 mph (137 km/h) to 97mph (156 km/h)

0-60mph (0-96 km/h): From 18.4sec to 14.1sec

In the 1100/1300, the engine was transversely-mounted, the cooling radiator being to one side of the engine bay.

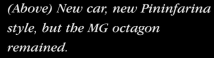

(Above) New car, new Pininfarina style, but the MG octagon remained.

(Left) The 1100's fascia/instrument display was simple, with a bank of switches alongside the strip speedometer (below).

(Left and Below) Although closely based on Austin/Morris 1100s, the MG version had its own specific identification.

1967-69 MGC

Although Austin-Healey was originally a rival sports car marque to MG, from the end of 1957 those cars were also assembled at Abingdon. The MG Midget of 1961 was a lightly-modified version of the latest Austin-Healey Sprite, and more such model-sharing could be expected in the future.

Accordingly, in the mid-1960s, when the time came to design a six-cylinder-engined replacement for the Austin-Healey 3000, MG's bosses at BMC considered producing not one, but two new cars, both to be based on the still-fresh MGB. Except that they would have had different front-end styles, and different badges, these two cars would have been the same. One was to be called MGC, and the other would be the Austin-Healey 3000 Mk IV. The Healey family, however, objected to the use of their name on a car

they had not designed, so the 'Austin-Healey' version was quietly dropped before the public got to know about it.

A new car called the MGC therefore appeared towards the end of 1967, and it was therefore no surprise to see that the old Austin-Healey 3000 was dropped at about the same time. Although the

Below: *To make space for the big engine, the MGC needed extra bulges in the hood pressing.*

MGC looked very similar to the up-dated MGB Mk II, the two cars were very different under the skin. Except for some of the outer panels, the MGC's front-end structure was completely different, for it had to accommodate a longer, much-heavier, six-cylinder engine. As before, open Roadster and fastback/hatchback GT versions of the same style were provided.

The engine itself was a 2,912cc unit, a complete re-design of the old Austin-Healey engine, and although lighter than before was very bulky. To accommodate this, MG provided a new type of independent front suspension, this having longitudinal torsion bars instead of coil springs, all tied to a new type of cross-member. This, in fact, was the first MG since 1950 to depart from the classic system first seen on the Y-Type sedans.

Behind the engine, MG provided not only a new and sturdy all-synchromesh gearbox, but the option of overdrive. In addition, there was also the option of fully-automatic (three-speed) transmission. Along with the sturdy Salisbury-type rear axle which was now to be standardised on all MGB-based models, this ensured a rugged, and long-lasting, power train.

Visually there was very little to make this car stand out from the MGB. MGCs were fitted with 15in. road wheels (the MGB had 14in. wheels), which caused the car to sit up slightly higher off the ground, and raised the overall gearing. To provide under-hood clearance for the longer and higher six-cylinder engine, there was a new hood pressing, which had a wide bulge towards the front, and an extra 'blip' above the front SU carburetor.

The MGC, as a concept, was a brave idea, which was rather let down by the detail, none of which was Abingdon's fault. If only the engine had been as light as the designers at BMC headquarters had originally promised, and if only it had produce the projected power and torque, the MGC would have handled better and would have been even faster.

As it was, the 120mph top speed was accompanied by a long-legged car which was much more of a fast tourer than a nimble sports car. Accordingly, it took time for the clientele to come to terms with this new type of MGB-based car. In fact the MGC was well-suited to the North American market, where speed limits were already being rigorously enforced. Although the automatic transmission option did not seem to sell quite as well as the company had hoped (along with the contemporary MGB Mk II, it was, after all, the very first automatic-transmission MG ever to be put on sale), it was well-suited to the torquey, low-revving engine, this producing a mechanical combination previously unknown behind an MG badge.

MILESTONE FACTS

- The MGC was the first six-cylinder model MG had built since 1939
- Although looking like the MGB, the MGC had a completely new front-end structure
- The MGC was the first MG to use torsion-bar suspension since the R-Type Midget of 1935
- The MGC's engine was shared with the Austin 3-Liter sedan of 1968 – 1971
- When announced, the MGC was the fastest road car MG had yet put on sale
- Along with the 1968MY MGB, the MGC was the first MG to be available with automatic transmission

Only weeks after the MGC was introduced (and when deliveries had only just begun), MG found itself part of the new British Leyland combine. Before long the planners behind that great conglomerate showed that they favoured Triumph, not MG, which meant that little development effort went into the MGC.

After one year, however, the engineers at Abingdon were allowed a complete rethink of the available transmissions, and ratios, so that what seemed to be a sluggish sports car (but was not, if the figures are to be believed) could be brightened up a little. For the 1969 Model Year the internal gearbox ratios and the axle ratios which were matched to 'overdrive' or 'non-overdrive' types were all re-shuffled, the result being that these then became the best of all MGCs.

Although sales held up well – nearly 9,000 cars would be assembled in less than two years – this was no better than had ever been achieved on the Austin-Healey 3000. British Leyland – not, please note, MG – therefore decided to cut out the still-young MGC, to allow Abingdon to concentrate on the MGB, for which demand was simply unending. In those two years, incidentally, there were 4,542 open-top Roadsters, and 4,457 MGC GTs. Peak production came in Calendar Year 1968, when 5,028 MGCs of both types were assembled. The last MGC was built only two years after it had been launched, and the six-cylinder engine was soon consigned to history. The special MGC-type body shell and torsion bar suspension was never used again. The next 'big-engined' MGB would not now appear until 1973, and be a very different type of car.

(Above)Only an expert can tell the difference between an MGC fascia (this one) and that of the contemporary MGB. (Left) 15in. wheels were used on the MGC, instead of the 14in. wheels used on the MGB.

TGT 72F

SPECIFICATIONS

Production: 8,999

Body styles: Two-seater Roadster or Coupe

Construction: Steel unit-construction body/chassis

Engine: Six-cylinders, 2,912cc.

Power Output: 145bhp

Transmission: Four-speed manual, optional overdrive, optional automatic

Suspension: Front – independent, coil springs, rear - beam axle, leaf springs

Brakes: Front discs, rear drums

Maximum speed: 120 mph (193 km/h)

0-60mph (0-96 km/h): 10.0sec

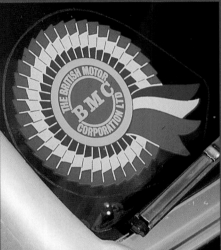

(Below) Nice touch added by the owner of this MGC – a sticker of BMC's noted trade mark roundel.

(Above) The MGC's engine was a bulky six-cylinder 2,912cc unit, much modified from that previously used in Austin-Healey 3000s.

1967-80 *MGB* MK II

After five years, the MGB was selling so well, particularly in North America, that MG saw no need to carry out a major re-design. The style was well-liked, and no consideration seems to have been given to a change in looks. An attempt to design a new car to take over from the Midget and the MGB (it was coded EX234, one car was built, and still exists) never found favor.

Instead, for the 1968 Model Year, MG turned the MGB into what the enthusiasts always called the 'Mk II'. Without altering the looks of this well-liked car, MG had worked hard at improving the chassis, and the optional equipment. Because the company was also about to introduce the closely-related six-cylinder-engined MGC, there was an opportunity to up-rate the main structure so that a new gearbox and (for the very first time on the MGB) an automatic transmission option could be made available. The very strong 'Salisbury' type axle which had first appeared on MGB GTs had just been standardised on all models too.

For 1968, therefore, the MGB gained a new and very robust four-speed all-synchromesh gearbox (this was to be shared with the much more powerful MGC), a box substantially more capable than the old B-Series box of the early cars. As before, Laycock overdrive was optional, but for the first time MG made Borg Warner automatic transmission an option. This, it was said, was to satisfy demand from the USA – though in the event it was never very popular in any market, and would be dropped after a very quiet six-year life.

Thus revised and improved, the MGB was exactly the sort of sports car which appealed to enthusiasts throughout the world – and particular in North America, where the MG legend had taken root, and would never be dislodged again. Other manufacturers tried to dislodge the MGB, but failed either on style, mechanical, or image grounds. MG, frustrated at times by the attitude of their British Leyland bosses (that final merger came in January 1968), continued to build on the MGB's reputation.

Not only did they build, and preserve, a peerless franchise network, but the long run of this model also ensured low selling and service costs. The MGB handled well, could be bought as an open or closed type, and was sufficient versatile to become a credible racing and (in European terms) rally car.

Once established, the MGB Mk II would push world-wide sales (and production at Abingdon) to new heights, this leaving every rival reeling. In 1969 no fewer than 31,030 MGBs were produced –

that figure exceeded the total of all MGs produced between 1924 and 1939, and also beat the all-time figure achieved by the TD In four seasons. But there was more to come – in 1972, before the latest American legislation had begun to lean so hard on the marque, Abingdon produced nearly 40,000 MGBs

Amazingly, until 1973 the MGB GT usually accounted for one third of all MGB production, for although it was heavier than the Roadster, it was also an extremely versatile car which could be used for fast driving, or as a comfortable commuting or suburban model.

By then, however, the MGB had been joined by another derivative, the MGB GT V8, and the pressure of North American legislation was becoming unbearable. In the seven years of life which remained for the MGB, the fight was always to keep abreast of the legislators, there being little time for real improvements.

From 1968, British Leyland authorised very few mechanical updates, but also imposed regular 'annual change' cosmetic improvements to make the MGB fresh for every spring-time assault on world markets. Rostyle wheels, reclining seats and a recessed grille arrived for 1970, a revised fascia for 1972, yet another grille for 1973, all accompanied by continual updates to trim, colour schemes, and fittings. Radial ply tires were finally standardised for all markets for 1974, while the slow-selling automatic transmission option was abandoned after 1973. The elegant MGB GT was finally withdrawn from the USA market at the end of 1973 – this fate also afflicting several other British Leyland sports cars at the same time.

Left: Over the years the MGB was facelifted persistently. This was a 1971/1972 model.

MILESTONE FACTS

- The MGB was by far the best-selling MG of all time.
- Without the rise of value of the british currency, MG sales in the USA were still profitable. Plans existed to keep it on sale until 1985.
- The MGB was the last car to be assembled at the Abingdon factory.
- By the late 1970s, USA emissions laws and strangled the MGB's engine, which could produce only 65bhp.
- From 1969 to 1973 the MGB was available with automatic transmission as optional equipment.
- The MGB GT was withdrawn from the US market after 1973, but sold strongly elsewhere until 1980.
- The MGB was the last-ever MG to be sold in the USA market

To meet the latest North American safety legislation, the biggest change of all arrived for the 1975 Model Year, when the MG was given vast black plastic fenders at front and rear. At the same time the chassis was raised to bring those fenders to a 'legal' height, and the engine for USA markets had to be de-tuned with a single (instead of twin) carburetors. The overdrive transmission was finally standardised on all cars in mid-1975 (though very few non-overdrive cars had been built for some time before this).

Since the MGB continued to sell very well, and there were no signs of a replacement being developed, there was still time for more change. For 1977 non-USA-market cars got a completely new fascia style, and although the suspension could not be lowered to its 'pre-1974' position, it was re-jigged and stiffened up to return the handling to the desired standards.

Sales began to ebb away in the late 1970s, but even in 1979, when Abingdon's eventual closure was forecast, more than 23,300 MGBs were produced. However, the end was near, for plans to fit the more modern (and much more powerful) British Leyland 'O' Series 2-liter engine were abandoned, and the last MGBs of all were produced in October 1980. The last cars of all, the 'LE' (Limited Edition) models, were marketed in 1981, but by this time demolition of the historic factory had already begun.

These were the last of all 'traditional' MGs. In 18 years, well over half-a-million MGBs of all types had been produced – this being a world record which was only breached by the Mazda Miata/MX-5 in the early 2000s.

(Above) Late model MGBs sold to the USA featured a single-carburetor engine like this.

(Left) The very last MGBs, produced at Abingdon in autumn 1980, were specially kitted out as 'Limited Edition' types.

(Above) *This was the fascia layout of the final 'Limited Edition' MGB of 1980.*
(Right) *Neat and to the point, with the reversing lamp inboard of the tail/turn indicator cluster.*

SPECIFICATIONS

Production: 375,147

Body styles: Two-seater Roadster, and Coupe

Construction: Steel, unit-construction body/chassis

Engine: Four-cylinders, 1,798cc.

Power Output: 95bhp at first (65bhp by late 1970s in North America)

Transmission: Four-speed manual, optional overdrive, optional automatic

Suspension: Front – independent, coil springs, rear - beam axle, leaf springs

Brakes: Front discs, rear drums

Maximum speed: 103 mph (166 km/h)

0-60mph (0-96 km/h): 12.2sec

(Right) *These five-spoke alloy wheels were standard on the 1980 LEs, but had been optional on earlier MGBs.*

1973-76 *MGB GT* V8

Although it took years to happen, one consequence of the formation of British Leyland was that companies which had once been rivals were encouraged to co-operate in joint ventures. One result was that engines from one company became available to another.

In the 1960s Rover had purchased the rights to building light-alloy (ex-Buick V8 engines from General Motors, and started fitting it into their own cars from 1967. From 1968 Rover became a constituent of British Leyland, and by the early 1970s they had to capacity to provide it to other British Leyland marques.

Well before Abingdon even thought of squeezing this bulky (though light) V8 into the MGB GT body shell, the same trick had been completed by an entrepreneur named Ken Costello. It was his success which prompted MG to develop their own 'official' version,

which went finally on sale in mid-1973. Purely for marketing reasons (there was no technical reason why the same transplant should not have been provided in the Roadster body shell), the Rover V8-engined MGB was only ever sold in GT guise: not only that, but because the engine had not then been 'federalized' for sale in the USA, every MGB GT was sold in Britain, and the

Below: *Wheels and badges were the only recognition points of the MGB GT V8, as introduced in 1973.*

American market never got the opportunity to sample this smooth, refined, super-fast and high-geared machine.

The combination was achieved in the most satisfactory way. First of all, MG took the 3.5-liter V8 from Rover, actually in slightly de-tuned 'Range Rover' guise. They then fitted their own specially-developed carburation and inlet manifolds, so that the twin SUs sat towards the rear of the engine bay, and were therefore not close to contacting the hood pressing.

Behind the engine, yet another version of the all-synchromesh four-speed gearbox was chosen (it had its own unique set of internal ratios), and Laycock overdrive was standard equipment. Because it was just about to be dropped from the four-cylinder MGB's options list, there was no surprise that automatic transmission was never available.

Although Abingdon's engineers were not allowed to make many visual changes in developing this car, they gained approval to use a new type of 14in cast-alloy road wheel, and there were discreet 'V8' badges on the front wings, and of course on the grille and trunk/hatchback lids themselves.

Here was one of the most attractive, and compellingly-attractive, MGs which had ever been put on sale. Not only was this the fastest MG road car of all time – officially it could reach 125mph, but many owners found that 130mph was possible in the most favourable of conditions – but its performance was delivered effortlessly, reliably, and with less fuss that from any previous MG. Although this derivative was, theoretically, less powerful than the obsolete MGC, every aspect of its performance was an improvement, Not only that, but an MGB GT V8 handled at least as well as a four-cylinder MGB GT, and never appeared to find any journey difficult.

And yet it did not sell at all well – especially after the end of 1974, when it inherited the same 'black fender' body style which had been added to all four-cylinder MGBs. One reason, for sure, was that here was a model only ever sold in one market – the UK – and in one body type – fastback/hatchback GT. Just by looking at other MGB-related models, we know that at least 80 per cent of all cars were sold in overseas markets, and that where all other market conditions were equal, that sat least two-thirds of all MGBs were open-top Roadsters.

By making only a few assumptions, we can guess that more than 30,000 V8-engined cars would have been sold in three years if they had enjoyed proper access to the world markets. Yet from mid-1973 to mid-1976, only 2,591 MGB GT V8s were sold, and on

MILESTONE FACTS

- The alloy V8 engine in the MGB GT V8 was original an American GM design, used in Buicks and related compact cars.

- Rover started building the MGB GT V8's engine in 1967. It powered many successful cars until 2003

- Although it measured 3.5-litrers, the V8 engine was no heavier than the other MGB power unit – the 1.8-liter 4-cylinder 'B-Series'

- The MGB GT V8 was sold only to British customers, in right-hand-drive form.

- In spite of the demand, MG would never sell the V8 in Roadster form.

- In 1973 the MGB GT V8 was the fastest MG Road car ever put on sale. It would not lose this title until 1992.

that basis here was a model which was never likely to be profitable.

Like the rival Triumph TR8 which was to arrive a few years later, the launch of the MGB GT V8 was desperately unlucky, for it arrived only weeks before the outbreak of the Yom Kippur War of 1973. Almost at a stroke, in retaliation, the OPEC nations quadrupled the price of crude oil, the price of fuel followed suit all over the world, and the sale of large engined cars plummeted. In the case of the MGB GT V8 this could certainly not be justified, as independent tests showed that it could return a day-to-day 25mpg (Imperial), which was very little worse than the equivalent four-cylinder MGB of the period. Sentiment, though, was not to be swayed by facts …

At the time, stories of engine supply shortages from Rover were allowed to take root, but these were not justified by the facts – especially as Rover car sales were also being hit by the same post-war hysteria. It was more likely that the MGB GT V8's high price was hitting it harder than MG would ever like to admit. In 1973, at launch, the first GT V8s were priced at £2,294 when a four-cylinder MGB GT cost only £1,547. Rival cars, especially the Ford Capri 3000GT (£1,824) also made the GT V8 look expensive, and this cannot have helped its progress.

After only three years, sales had fallen away so far that only 176 cars were produced in Calendar Year 1976. It was inevitable, really, that the most accomplished of all MGB-derivative models would be discontinued, which left Abingdon full – and it still was very full – of only two cars – the four-cylinder MGB and the little Midget.

(Above) The Rover V8 engine fitted snugly into the MGB engine bay – though the carburetors had to be located at the rear of the unit.

(Left) These alloy wheels were standard equipment on the MGB GT V8.

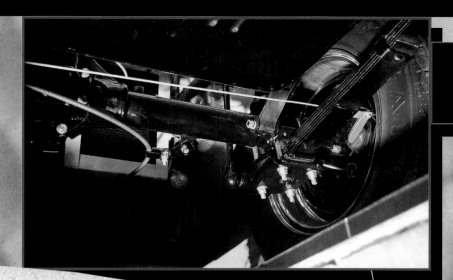

(Left) Twin SU carburetors fed the V8 engine through long and complex manifolding.

Simple rear suspension, by half-elliptic leaf springs, with lever arm dampers, in the MGB GT V8.

SPECIFICATIONS

Production: 2,591

Body styles: Two-seater GT coupe

Construction: Steel unit-construction body/chassis

Engine: V8-cylinders, 3,528cc.

Power Output: 137bhp

Transmission: Four-speed manual, with overdrive

Suspension: Front – independent, coil springs, rear - beam axle, leaf springs

Brakes: Front discs, rear drums

Maximum speed: 124 mph (200 km/h)

0-60mph (0-96 km/h): 8.6sec

PVH 556M

1982-90 *Metro* & *Metro Turbo*

By 1980, the MG marque was in disarray. The Midget was killed off in 1979, BL (the parent company) announced that Abingdon was soon to close, and October 1980 the last MGB of all was assembled. For a very short time it looked as if an MG badged version of the Triumph TR7 might be produced, but fortunately that idea was speedily abandoned.

Franchise dealers, particular in the USA, were distraught, for it soon became quite clear that no new MG sports cars were under development. MG, as a marque, actually disappeared for a time, but in 1982 the first tentative steps to rebirth followed. First came a car called the MG Metro, and the Metro Turbo soon followed it.

Having concluded that they could not make money by building sports cars, BL's bean counters elected to start building sporty sedans and hatchbacks again. As in the days of MG1100 and MG1300 types, these would be based on an Austin-badged family car, and would have transversely-mounted engines driving the front wheels.

The difference, though, was that the new car, called the MG Mini Metro, would be the very first MG to have a hatchback body style, the first to use BL's latest 'floating on air' Hydragas suspension system – and it would also be the very first MG to be assembled at the Longbridge factory, BL's headquarters complex

Below: *The MG Metro revived the MG badge in 1982, the turbocharged version being an even faster derivative.*

just to the south of Birmingham. The Mini Metro, originally described as BL's 'make or break' car, had taken years to evolve, for originally it had been meant to replace the Mini, but had grown up to be significantly larger. Even so, the same basic layout (as the Mini and the 1100/1300) was retained, though with high-compression gas being used instead of a water/alcohol mix as a vital element in the suspension.

Compared with the Austin Metro, which had engines of 41bhp and 63bhp, the MG version was boosted to 72bhp, which delivered a top speed of just 100mph. This was the minimum which BL thought they could offer on an MG-badged hatchback in the 1980s. Changes to the trim, the interior equipment, and of course with the provision of MG badging, all helped to convince the clientele that this little car was a worthy bearer of the octagon badge.

And, if you ignored the cars, pedigree, so it was. Under the skin it might indeed be based on an Austin runabout, but it was brisk if not super fast, it handled very well indeed, and because it sold for only £4,799 in 1982, it offered good value. It wasn't meant to be a sports car, and it wasn't meant to get into motorsport – but it offered that important bit of 'class' which buyers seemed to want.

Only months after the MG Metro was launched, BL surprised everyone by adding an even faster, more specialized version to the range – the Metro Turbo. Not only did this new type have no less than 93bhp, but it was the very first MG-badged car to be fitted with a turbocharged engine.

Because the Metro engine bay was so compact, a great deal of ingenuity had been needed to squeeze a turbocharger into a restricted area. Because BL's engineering team at Longbridge was currently over-burdened with the development of other, more mundane, new cars, this new model programme had to be contracted out. To sort out a viable package, and to make sure that the extra heat generated by a turbocharger could be managed, BL hired the Lotus company to do the job. Lotus not only built its own sports cars, but had a rapidly expanding consultancy division, who treated this as a real challenge.

Although the position of the transversely-mounted MG Metro engine was not changed, Lotus somehow found space to instal a Garrett AiResearch T3 turbocharger behind the cylinder block, close to a single SU carburetor. Sounds simple, really, but because of the known limits of the existing in-the-sump transmission, Lotus was obliged to limit the amount of power which could developed.

MILESTONE FACTS

- The MG badge was dormant in 1981, and early 1982. The Metro was the first new-generation MG to bring the marque back to life.

- The Metro Turbo was the first MG to use a turbocharged engine. Two other turbo-MGs, the Maestro Turbo and Montego Turbo models, would follow it in the 1980s.

- The Metro's engine was basically the same as that of the 1960s/1970s Midget sports car.

- The Metro was MG's first-ever hatchback model.

- The Metro was the first-ever MG to be assembled at the historic Longbridge factory

- The 200-off MG Metro 6R4 was very loosely based on the layout of the original Metro, though it had a V6 engine in the tail, and four-wheel-drive.

- Once version of the Metro carried large octagon decals on its sides – these were the largest octagons ever found on a road car.

Although the sturdy 1,275cc engine could certainly have produced a lot more power, therefore, its showroom limit was set at a mere 93bhp. 'Works' race cars, with special transmissions, regularly raced with at least twice that power output.

Even so, this was quite enough to give the spritely little car a top speed of more than 110mph, and work on the chassis (which included stiffening up the suspension and altering the front-end geometry) meant that this was a very capable little sports hatchback.

Except for tiny details – alloy wheels and low-profile tires, brake-cooling vents in the front spoiler, and of course in the colour schemes and badging – a Metro Turbo looked like an MG Metro, so many owners could surprise other motorists with the sheer pace of what looked quite ordinary.

Although MG die-hards initially fought against everything which these Metros set out to do, the sales figure proved that they were in a tiny minority. Not only did the Metro re-introduced MG to the market place. In eight difficult years – years in which BL, which became Austin-Rover, and which later became the Rover Group, battled to stay in business - no fewer than 142,175 MG-badged Metros were produced, which made it a commercial success by any standard. It was, however, perhaps a touch too small, so it remains the smallest modern-type MG ever to be put on sale.

SPECIFICATIONS

Model: Metro and Metro Turbo

Production: 142,175

Body styles: Three-door hatchback

Construction: Steel unit-construction body/chassis

Engine: Four- cylinders, 1,275cc.

Power Output: 72bhp/93bhp

Transmission: Four-speed manual

Suspension: Front – independent, Hydragas, rear – independent, Hydragas

Brakes: Front discs, rear drums

Maximum speed: 100mph (161 km/h)/111mph (179 km/h)

0-60mph (0-96 km/h): 12.2sec/9.4sec

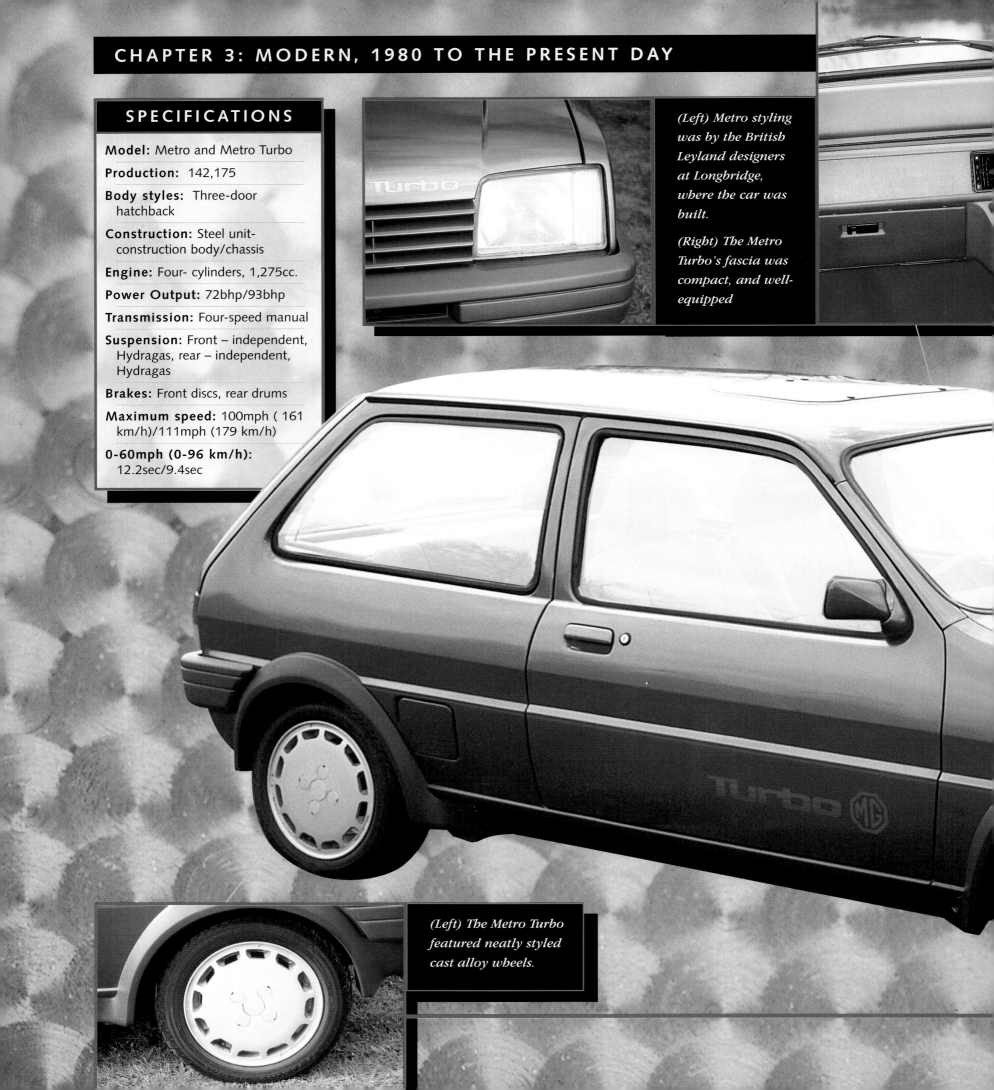

(Left) Metro styling was by the British Leyland designers at Longbridge, where the car was built.

(Right) The Metro Turbo's fascia was compact, and well-equipped

(Left) The Metro Turbo featured neatly styled cast alloy wheels.

(Right) All Metros and Turbos featured transversely-mounted A-Series engines. The turbocharger on this car is hidden away under the carburetor.

Front-end detail on the Metro Turbo, with a spoiler intended to smooth out the aerodynamic flow under the nose.

1992-95 *MG RV8*

Although the MG marque survived the 1980s, and very profitably too, the badge did not appear on any of the sports cars that originally made the name so famous. Instead it was Metros, larger Maestros and even larger Montegos – all of then being tuned-up and more specialised derivatives of front-wheel-drive Austins – which kept the flame alive.

BL which somehow survived a torrid commercial decade, eventually became the Rover Group, then took a strategic decision to revive the fortunes of MG. To do this it elected to start by producing a short-life derivative of the ancient MG, then after a period of soul searching (and the need to find a commercial partner) to introduce an all-new model.

But how could the new short-life model, called RV8 but based on the old MGB Roadster, ever be manufactured ? That, after all, was a model which had breathed its last in 1980, in a factory which

Below: *Although the RV8 was based on the structure of the old MGB, almost every exterior panel had been reshaped.*

had been razed to the ground almost immediately afterwards. The secret was that all the press tooling and assembly fixtures for the MGB had somehow been preserved – and, in fact 'new' body shells were once again being built by the end of the 1980s. These were being produced, in small but significant numbers, at a small facility close to the old Abingdon site.

By any standards, this was an indulgence, a hasty indulgence at that, but Rover was determined to pave the way for more important MG sports cars, and this, they concluded, was the only practical method. Using a dedicated corner of the much-modernised Cowley factory (this had originally been the Pressed Steel body plant which had supplied Morris for many years), Rover set out to build a much-changed derivative of the old MGB Roadster.

In some ways this was the car which MG should have produced in the mid-1970s (but they had only been allowed to build GT V8 coupes), but in other ways the modifications were carried too far. Starting with the basic structure of the old MGB Roadster, the stylists added flared front and rear wheel-arches, sills under the doors, and a lengthened nose which featured different-style headlamp pods, and extra driving lamps. All these changes were incorporated into new shells to be built by the Heritage concern – which meat that shells for original-type MGBs were not available for some time. The interior, totally revised, had squashy seats, and a new wooden fascia with a full display of instruments.

Under the skin, Rover provided the latest 3.9-liter version of the venerable light-alloy V8 engine, virtually in contemporary Range Rover tune, which produced 190bhp and no less than 231lb.ft of torque. Matched by an old-type Rover five-speed transmission, and with a big burly solid rear axle, it was a rock solid drive line.

By comparison, there were really few changes to the old chassis, for the RV8 still retained rear-wheel drum brakes, and the rear axle was suspended on half-elliptic leaf springs, though extra location links were provided. Two other modernisation features included the use of telescopic (not lever arm) shocks at front and rear, along with anti-sway bars to help firm-up the handling. The suspension package was topped off by 205/65-15in. tires on lattice-style cast-alloy road wheels.

It was an interesting, if definitely 'Retro' package – both mechanically and visually – and it only needed a short drive to convince the driver that this was not a car of the 1990s, but a good (and very powerful) example of the 1970s. Everything which had been going out of motoring style in the 1970s – including the hard ride and the cramped cabin – was still present, though the much higher

MILESTONE FACTS

- The RV8 of 1992 was the first MG sports car to have been built since 1980
- The RV8 was loosely based on the structure of the old MGB Roadster
- Bodies for the RV8 were built by British Motor heritage, a small Faringdon-based business which was servicing the classic car restoration industry.
- The majority of RV8s were sold in Japan.
- The RV8 was only ever built in right-hand-drive form.
- The gearbox of the RV8 was a five-speeder originally designed for use in the Rover SD1 executive hatchback.
- RV8s were assembled at Cowley – the first ever to be built in the much-modernised factory complex, which now assembles MINIs.

performance (the top speed was 136mph) compensated for a lot.

Although launch came in October 1992, the first deliveries were made early in 1993. What might be called 'traditional' MG enthusiasts seemed to be impressed, but few of them seemed to be willing to pay the high price of £25,440 which was asked. Rover's problem was that old-style MGT GT V8's, superbly restored, could be bought for half that price, and were seen as more pure examples of this model's lengthy evolution.

Rover, therefore, had a commercial problem. More sales would follow a price reduction, but that could only come if more cars could be built – and that was not possible. Production was limited by the number of body shells which could be supplied from British Motor Heritage – 25 a week was stretching their resources to the limit – and unit costs could not be driven down unless that rate could be pushed up. It never was. Then there was the limit on where this car could be sold, for it may be significant that no attempt was ever made to engineer this car for sale in the USA – in fact only right-hand steering types were ever manufactured.

In the end, more than half of all the 2,000 RV8s ever built were exported to Japan, where there seemed to be a very healthy regard for MG-badged sports cars. Even so, after only two years, this intriguing anachronism was quietly abandoned, the Heritage business returned to building shells for old-style MGBs, and the special facility at Cowley was put to other use.

The next MG, launched at the same time, was the MGF, which had nothing in common with the RV8.

(Above) Serious stuff – on the RV8 the speedometer was calibrated up to 140mph.
(Left) The RV8's engine was a descendant of that used in the MGB GT V8, but now a 3.9-liter with fuel injection.

New body style, but no change to the legendary octagon badge.

(Right) The RV8's fascia/instrument panel was all-new, a neat combination of modern style and retro materials.

SPECIFICATIONS

Production: 2,000

Body styles: Two-seater Roadster

Construction: Steel, unit construction body/chassis

Engine: V8-cylinders, 3,946cc.

Power Output: 190bhp

Transmission: Five-speed manual

Suspension: Front – independent, coil springs, rear - beam axle, leaf springs

Brakes: Front discs, rear drums

Maximum speed: 136 mph (219 km/h)

0-60mph (0-96 km/h): 6.9sec

(Left) Although the detail was different, the RV8 retained the semi-recessed headlamp layout of the original MGB.

1995-2002 MGF

One of the bravest decisions ever made by the Rover Group in the early 1990s was to approve the development of a new mid-engined MG sports car. History now tells us that this car, the MGF, was a commercial success, but we may never know just how vital was the decision to make this a joint project with the makers of the body structures, Mayflower of Coventry.

In fact the MGF's future was by no means settled in 1994, when BMW took control of Rover – but the German concern speedily gave approval for development to be completed.

In many ways the shape, form and layout of the MGF was influenced by existing sports cars like the Toyota MR2, and by a previous icon, the Fiat X1/9. In all cases these cars featured a transversely-mounted engine, which was positioned behind a two-seater cabin, and drove the rear wheels. In each case, this was done because a suitable transverse-engine front-wheel-drive package already existed in one of the company's family hatchbacks.

Once a mid-engined layout had been chosen, the general packaging of the MGF virtually chose itself. Using a 93.5in/2,375mm wheelbase (that of the 1970s Midget, for comparison, had been 80in./2,032mm and that of the MGB had been 91in/2,311mm), Rover evolved a simple and rugged steel monocoque body-chassis structure, which would require major new investment in tooling and assembly facilities. Almost all the running, gear,

Below: *Cutaway showing the mid engine layout*

though, was lifted from existing Rover family hatchbacks.

To make the bodies, at a planned rate of not more than 10,000 cars a year, Rover then joined forces with the Mayflower Group of Coventry, whose Motor Panels business was already an accomplished operator in the body stamping, welding, and assembling business. In this case, however, Mayflower also took a Brave Pill, by agreeing to share the commercial risk – they would pay for their own body tooling if they could also share in the profits to be made from the new venture. This was vital to the success of the MGF, for Rover later admitted that they could not otherwise have found the capital from their own resources.

On the original cars, the mid-mounted engine was a 1.8-liter version of Rover's celebrated 16-valve K-Series power unit (as used in many other Rover models), and was available in 118bhp or 143bhp guise, but over the years an entry-level 1.6-liter/112bhp engine was offered, as also was a 158bhp version of the 1.8-liter unit. The gearbox was that used in Rover 200/Rover 400 hatchbacks, and a few 'Tiptronic-change' style CVT-equipped cars were also sold, though these were very rare indeed. Incidentally, access to the engine for normal servicing was very restricted indeed – there was a hinged panel in the body, behind the seats – and Rover made it clear that this MG should be maintained by a franchise dealer.

For suspension and steering, the MGF leaned heavily on the Rover 100 (the re-developed Rover/MG Metro hatchback), which is to say that there was independent suspension at front and rear, with suspension (MG Metro-style) by the latest interconnected Hydragas units. A new type of speed-sensitive electric power-assisted steering was standardised, and naturally there were four-wheel-disc brakes.

Although the MGF took over from the RV8 in the showrooms there was, of course, absolutely no connection between the two. The MGF was exactly what the clientele had been asking for – in fact if MG's fortunes had been more robust in the 1970s an earlier derivative of this layout might even have been built at Abingdon. This, though, was a car which relied on Rover engineering at Longbridge, and it became the first MG sports car to be assembled at the Longbridge plant. Sales began in mid-1995, and proved remarkably buoyant through the often turbulent times suffered by Rover in this period.

For the first time in many years, the planners got the image of an MG exactly right. The new model looked smooth and distinctive – it had a rounded nose, a stubby tail, a comfortable and well-equipped

MILESTONE FACTS

- The MGF was the first mid-engined MG sports car to go on sale
- The MGF was the first MG to use the much-acclaimed 16-valve twin-cam Rover K-Series engine.
- The MGF was the first MG sports car to be assembled at Longbridge.
- Although it would have been an ideal car to sell in the USA, no MGF ever reached US shores
- From 1995 to 2001, the MGF was the only model keeping the MG marque alive.
- During the life of the MGF, a CVH type of automatic transmission became optional. Very few were ever sold.
- MGF suspensions were interconnected, front to rear, by the Hydragas installation.

cabin, and of course it included all the latest 'must-haves' including anti-lock braking, power-assisted steering, and the availability of air conditioning – and it certainly exuded a great deal of character.

Although some pundits wondered why it could not feel more 'nervous' on the road – the MGF was first, last, and above all an understeering car – there was universal praise for its rattle-free build quality, for the sheer charm and ability of the high-revving twin-cam engines, for the supple ride, and for the ample supply of sports car character.

In many ways the MGF was superior to anything which had ever been built at Abingdon – it was faster, smarter, softer-riding, and better built – and at the same time it was a thoroughly civilised two-seater. Although a smart and rather rounded drop-on hardtop was an option, this was not sold in huge qualities, for most MGF customers seemed to want their cars to have the top down as often as possible.

The only clientele dissatisfied by the new MGF were in North America, for Rover had made a conscious decision not to sell the new car in that market: simply, it was not to be made available in a continent where more than 300,000 MGBs had been delivered. For that, enthusiasts could only blame their own legislators, for it was the sheer cost and complication of meeting modern legislation which kept MG out of its once-dominant market as the twenty-first century opened.

Even so, the MGF sold well, and fast, in most other continents. In 2002 it was still yet seen as old-fashioned when it was replaced by a much-improved derivative, the MG TF.

(Above) The MGF's driving compartment featured airbags ahead of driver and passenger.

(Above) Nice touch – the key-operated, flush-mounted, filler cap.

(Far Left) In the MGF, the engine was not easy to get it through an access panel in the shroud, behind the seats.

(Left) Five-spoke alloy wheels, with a unique style, on the MGF

Same badge, no style changes. No MG enthusiast needed to be reminded, surely?

SPECIFICATIONS

Production: 77,269

Body styles: Two-seater Roadster

Construction: Steel, unit-construction body/chassis

Engine: Four-cylinders, 1,589cc/1,796cc.

Power Output: 112bhp/118bhp/143bhp/158bhp

Transmission: Five-speed manual

Suspension: Front – independent, Hydragas, rear – independent, Hydragas

Brakes: Front discs, rear discs

Maximum speed: 120mph (193km/h)/123 mph (198 km/h)/130mph (209 km/h)/137mph (220 km/h)

0-60mph (0-96 km/h): 8.7sec/7.6sec

2001- MG ZR

In 1994 the Rover Group was purchased by BMW, who spent six years trying to make the company profitable. When this strategy failed, BMW sold off Rover for a mere £10 ($17), and wrote off the massive outstanding debts, to a buy out team which lacked capital to spend on new models.

The new team, led by John Towers (a previous CEO of Rover), elected to brighten up the product line by developing MG-badged versions of existing Rover products.

The MG ZR, therefore, which went on sale in mid-2001, was a lightly modified version of the Rover 25, a family hatchback with some earlier connection with Honda models which had shared platforms and running gear in the 1990s. There was no connection with any previous MG model although, like the MGF sports car, this new range was to be assembled in the same factory at Longbridge.

The thinking behind the ZR was similar to that which had supported earlier MG sedans and hatchbacks. Although the basic design, structure and running gear would be closely based on that of a mass-market model (in this case the 25), there would be

unique differences in front-end style, in the handling characteristics, and in the equipment of the MG version. Although this might sound easy to achieve, and facile in its reasoning, as far as the clientele was concerned it was desirable. Within three years the sale of MG-badged cars was matching that of Rover-badged cars in some market sectors.

To finalise this car very rapidly – it was previewed within a year of Rover being sold off by BMW, and was on sale within 15 months – one important decision taken by the new management was that the ZR should share exactly the same range of engine/transmission

Below: *The first of the 2000s-generation MGs was the front-wheel-drive ZR, based on the Rover 25.*

options as the Rover 25. Accordingly, along with the larger ZT, which was launched at the same time, the ZR became the first-ever MG-based car for which a diesel-engined option was available.

Although this might sound like an enormous dilution of the MG pedigree, market forces (particularly in Continental Europe, where diesel prices were much lower) could not be ignored. Every major car maker in Europe offered diesel-engined versions of its products, and in some countries more diesel, than petrol, cars were being sold. There was no shame, therefore in owning a ZR diesel, especially as the turbocharged engines had more low-speed torque than any petrol version, and it might cruise at up to 100mph where conditions, and the law, allowed.

The ZR range was based on the same transversely-mounted, front-engine, front-wheel-drive package as the Rover 25, and was sold only as a three-door hatchback. All the petrol-engined models used one or other of Rover's celebrated 16-valve twin-overhead-camshaft K-Series power unit, the smallest being a 102bhp/1.4-liter, and the most powerful being the same 160bhp/1.8-liter unit which was fitted to contemporary versions of the MGF sports car.

The turbo-diesel version was Rover's versatile 2-liter L-Series, which had eight valves and a single overhead camshaft cylinder head. By 2001 it had already been used in cars as different as the Rover 600 saloon and the Land Rover Freelander, and although it was heavy, it delivered mountains of torque and adequate power.

Under the skin, the rest of the chassis was conventional enough, with independent suspension by coil springs at front and rear (MacPherson struts up front, and a torsion beam at the rear), and with nicely-weighted power-assisted rack-and-pinion steering. All in all, this was a compact car – it was only 156in/3973mm long – and its appeal was enhanced because it was just one of a range of three new MG-badged Rovers – the ZR, medium-sized ZS and large ZT types.

The ZR was received warmly by MG enthusiasts, especially as there had not been any modern-specification MG sedans or hatchbacks on sale for a decade. Although MG-Rover never tried to hide the origins of the new ZR, the new derivative was different enough, and special enough, for it to be recognised as worthy to carry the octagon badge. The front-end style was a new evolution on tradition, with a MG-like grille recessed into front-end sheet metal which was otherwise the same as that of the Rover 25. Maybe the high-mounted spoiler on the hatchback – it was really an extension of the roof – did little for the aerodynamic performance, but it made yet another statement about this new model's intent.

MILESTONE FACTS

- The ZR hatchback was a close relative of the Rover 25 model
- The ZR/25 models were both evolutions of a front-wheel-drive hatchback which had been inspired by Honda in the 1990s
- Along with other Z-Series MG, the Zr was the very first to be offered with the option of a diesel engine
- In 2003, MG-Rover announced a delivery van version of the ZR – this was the very first time that such a body style had been offered behind an MG badge.
- The ZR was developed immediately after BMW had sold the Rover combine. BMW had not wished to produce cars like this, which might compete with their own sports sedans.
- Much-modified ZRs became successful in British rallying.

Inside the cabin, although it felt like a slightly cramped four-seater (this was really a package which had been first finalised in the early 1990s, after all, and standards had changed) there was a nicely-equipped fascia/instrument board, with black-lettering-on-white-background instruments. Wide-rim light-alloy road wheels were standard throughout.

In character, for sure, the ZR delivered well, for every version of the K-Series engine revved very cleanly and eagerly. The 160bhp type helped the ZR to a top speed of more than 130mph (this was a lot higher than MG-badged hatchbacks of ten years earlier), and every independent road tester was delighted with the handling and balance of the new model. In the UK, too, the pricing was right – for ZR prices started at only £9,995. A 160bhp ZR (the one which most enthusiasts wanted, even if they could not justify it to the bank manager) cost £14,345, which was considerably less than that asked for the main rivals.

Sales bloomed almost at once, and before long MG was selling tens of thousands of these cars every year. There is no doubt that this was the sensible, pragmatic, way to re-launch the MG badge in closed-top form, and there is also no doubt that it helped to keep the business alive at Longbridge while other, and more exciting, MGs, were being developed.

To prove their point, MG-Rover encouraged the development of 'works' rally cars, where the 1.6-liter derivative proved to be class competitive, and proved beyond doubt that the structure and Rover-based chassis was rugged, reliable and versatile in all conditions.

SPECIFICATIONS

Production: Introduced 2001

Body styles: Three-door hatchback

Construction: Steel unit construction body/chassis

Engine: Four-cylinders, 1,396cc/1,589cc/1,796cc/Diesel 1,994cc .

Power Output: 102bhp/115bhp./160bhp/101bhp /113bhp

Transmission: **Five-speed manual**

Suspension: Front – independent, coil springs, rear – independent, coil springs

Brakes: Front discs, rear discs

Maximum speed: 108 mph (174 km/h) to 131mph (211 km/h)

0-60mph (0-96 km/h): 10.0sec to 7.8 sec

(Left) Neat alloys on the new front-drive ZR.

(Above) The 16-valve
twin-cam K-Series
engine of the ZR was
closely related to that
used in the MGF.

(Above) ZR styling
was by Peter Stevens,
who had earlier
shaped the McLaren
F1 road car.

2001- *MG ZT*

As already mentioned in describing the ZR hatchback, the revived Rover company, soon to be re-titled MG-Rover for obvious marketing reasons, elected to introduced not one, but three totally different new MG cars in 2001 – ZR, ZS and ZT – all of them being based on Rover products which were already on sale.

The marketing strategy, which soon proved to be triumphantly correct, was to cover a big section of the market-place with MG-badged sports sedans and hatchbacks. Like the other new MGs (ZR and ZS), the ZT was to be assembled among its sister Rover models at Longbridge, where all MG assembly was now concentrated.

The ZT model – originally available only as a four-door sedan, but later to be joined by an impressive, and equally intriguing wagon version (called ZT-T) – was the largest, fastest and most prestigious of these new cars. This was emphasised by the fact that UK prices started at £18,595, and that one of the engine produced 190bhp.

Like the other 2001-generation MG tin-tops, the ZT had its origins in an existing Rover model, this being the 75 sedan. Unlike the smaller new MGs, this particular Rover had been conceived, tested, and put into production entirely under BMW ownership, which meant that the German company could impose many of its own standards. Previewed in 1998, and available in numbers from 1999, the new Rover was badged '75', which revived a much-loved model title of the 1950s and 1960s.

Although it was inspired by BMW, the engineering and running gear of the Rover 75 was almost entirely British, though the manual gearbox was by Getrag, which was already very well-connected with BMW. As expected, the roomy engine bay was arranged to accept a whole variety of transversely-mounted petrol and diesel engines, with a choice of manual or automatic transmission, and naturally this philosophy was carried forward to the launch of the newly-badged MG ZT.

Although the front-end style was modified to accept what MG enthusiasts soon came to recognise as the corporate MG 'face'; the rest of the smoothly-detailed four-door sedan style, and its amazingly rigid monocoque structure, was carried forward unchanged. Naturally the new car also had alloy wheels, a boot-lid-mounted rear spoiler, and a choice of positively extrovert color schemes.

Right: *MG's ZT-T was the very first wagon bodied MG evere to go on sale.*

Like the Rover 75, the MG ZT was made available with two types of petrol engine, and one turbo-diesel. The entry-level ZT used a 115bhp/1.8-liter version of the 16-valve K-Series, the same basic power unit as already found in the ZR, ZS and MGF models, but the most stirring versions used the compact, powerful and high-revving KV6 – a 24-valve 60-degree V6 engine which was also a part of the K-Series family. Not only was this 2.5-liter engine immediately

available with the normal 160bhp, but 177bhp was matched to automatic transmission, and there was also a mildly tuned-up version with 190bhp.

Soon after launch, this MG was also offered with a four-cylinder turbo-diesel engine, this being the 115bhp/1,951cc BMW power unit which already powered the Rover 75, the Land Rover Freelander, and many small and medium sized BMWs. Not only that, but a higher-powered, 131bhp, derivative soon appeared – this being enough to propel a ZT up to 120mph.

Although it would have been easy for MG-Rover to make the new cars into a dreadful pastiche of what a high-performance sedan should be, most testers found that the ZT combined many virtues. Unless one ordered it in one of the more extrovert colors (some people wondered how a bright-yellow car like this could possibly sell ?) the

MILESTONE FACTS
• The ZT was evolved from the Rover 75 executive sedan. This was a car designed during BMW's ownership of the Rover Group.
• The ZT-T was a wagon version of the ZT – the very first MG badged wagon ever to go on sale.
• One version of the ZT had a V6 engine, this being the first time a series-production V6-engined Rover had gone on sale.
• Diesel-powered versions of the ZT used a BMW power unit – this being the first, and only, time such a make of engine has been used in an MG.
• The ZT was one of three Rover-based cars, all introduced by MG-Rover in the summer of 2001.

ZT always looked rock-solid and purposeful. Not only that, but this was a car which seemed to be built to higher quality standards than any previous MG. BMW's legacy to Rover, which they ditched after only six years, was that they instilled new high standards of building.

Here, therefore, was not only the quickest, largest, MG ever – a 190bhp KV6-engined ZT could reach 140mph, comfortably, quickly, and in great style – but one which rode softly, which seemed to have eliminated all road noise from the interior, and which was by no means as costly as originally feared.

As Britain's Autocar magazine pointed out, after testing the new model : 'The ZT makes MG-Rover a formidable contender in this competitive market. It is a tribute to Rover's engineering that it has produced such convincing yet different cars from such similar underpinnings.'

The ZT, in other words, was the sort of car which MG should have made in previous decades, but had never managed it. Way back in the 1930s, an SA or a WA was brisk and elegant, but never all that well built. In the 1960s, the 1100s and the Magnettes were too closely based on Austin sedan. Now, for the new century, great care had gone into re-jigging a modern family car – and it seemed to have worked.

In the 1980s cars like the MG Maestro and MG Montego seemed to have been too cynically developed, but this new ZT was well on the way to having its own character. There was so much poise, and so much potential, in the chassis, that MG's very first wagon– the ZT-T – was added to the range. By 2003, with the range further fleshed out by the much-different ZT 260V8, no fewer than 19 sub-derivatives were listed.

SPECIFICATIONS

Production: Introduced in 2001

Body styles: Four-door sedan/wagon

Construction: Steel unit-construction body/chassis

Engine: Four-cylinders, 1,796cc/V6-cylinders, 2,497cc/Diesel, 4-cylinder 1,951cc.

Power Output: 115bhp to 190bhp

Transmission: Five-speed manual, optional automatic

Suspension: Front – independent, coil springs, rear – independent, coil springs

Brakes: Front discs, rear discs

Maximum speed: 120 mph (193 km/h) to 140mph (225 km/h)

0-60mph (0-96 km/h): 11.0sec to 8.5sec

(Above) Though based on the Rover 75, the ZT had its own style of fascia/instrumentation.

(Top page, center) Four-wheel disc brakes, behind cast alloy wheels, were standard equipment on ZT models.

MG advertised the ZT as the fastest MG yet put on sale – which it was, until 2003.

(Above) One of the ZT and ZT-T power units was the compact 2.5-liter KV-6 engine, always allied to front-wheel-drive.

(Right) Even on a modern executive saloon, the MG octagon was always present.

2002- *MG TF*

More than six years after the mid-engined MGF had gone on sale, MG was finally ready to up-date the design still further. Without the well-publicised financial problems which afflicted the parent company (Rover, later MG-Rover), such changes might have been made somewhat earlier.

Not that there had ever been any complaints from the clientele, for up to 15,000 examples of MGF were still being made every year – and this was without any attempt being made to market cars in the USA.

MG-Rover finally announced a much-improved the car, badging it MG TF (which was only slightly confusing with the last of the traditional MG sports cars, which had last been built in 1955). Although the basis of the car was the MGF, the engineers and marketing whiz-kids had been able to re-work it, and improve it, in many ways.

As with all new models being developed by the cash-strapped MG-Rover Group at this time, this had to be a project to be completed with a modest capital outlay. Accordingly, the TF still used the basic body shell of the now-obsolete MGF, though cosmetic, and some sheet-metal, changes had been made at the front, rear and the sides. In the process, too, the structure had been stiffened up, but Mayflower was still able to build these cars without making too many changes to the assembly fixtures in Coventry. Design director Peter Stevens (he was also responsible for the new ZR/ZS/ZT models too) had achieved much without breaking the bank.

Below: *The TF of 2002 was a comprehensive re-think of the original MGF design*

Visually, therefore, the TF differed from the MGF by having a longer and rather more shapely snout, one which carried a new facsimile of an MG grille, and which now had fashionable headlamp pods containing four smaller lamps, with the turn indicators also housed under the same glass. The new front fender molding had a much larger air scoop than before. Changes at the rear were less pronounced, for the expensive-to-replace tail lamp clusters and the existing engine lid/trunk lid had not been changed (though the spoiler 'flip' as featured on previous MGF Trophy models, had been standardised). Under them, however, there was a new fender molding which matched the new front-end style. There were new under-door sill pressings, and changes had also been made to the rear wings.

Although the engine line up stayed basically the same – the 'entry-level' 1.6-liter engine produced 114bhp, the most highly-tuned 1.8-liter produced 158bhp – what was expected to be the best-selling 1.8-liter unit had been boosted to 135bhp as did the choice of five-speed manual transmission, and (very rarely found) the CVT-type automatic option.

The major chassis change was to the suspension, where the expensive old interconnected Hydragas suspension (whose origins were way back in the British Leyland of the 1970s) had been abandoned, in favour of conventional coil spring-over-telescopic damper units. Not only that, but at the rear there was a new type of linkage for the independent rear suspension. Now there was no interconnection between front and rear suspensions. The whole, MG-Rover insisted at the time of launch, was that the TF was now an out-and-out sports car which would feel more exciting to drive.

Although MG also brought in a price increase at the same time – from 2002 TF prices started at £15,750 for the 1.6-liter car, while the 1.8-liter/160bhp car sold for £19,995 – this was a tiny increment that brought no resistance from the likely customers. What was important to MG was that here, for the first time since 1995, was a car which looked visually different – and this meant that existing MGF owners could trade in/trade-up without being disappointed by their new car.

Somehow or other, design director Peter Stephens's team had made a very compact car look considerably larger and more impressive without actually adding much bulk, and virtually no weight. Naturally the wheelbase, cabin and general structure had not changed, and either had the width, nor the rear overhang. It was only at the front where there was a mere 1.15in/29mm of extra length. Visual tricks, however, had done a lot to make this two-seater look even more impressive than the car it replaced.

MILESTONE FACTS

- In 2002, the launch of the TF revived an MG model name which had last been used 47 years earlier. Technically, of course, there was no connection between the two cars.

- The TF was a substantial redesign of the the MGF, for which it was a direct replacement.

- Compared with the MGF, the new TF used conventional steel coil springs; there was no interconnection between front and rear suspension systems.

- The TF was the first MG sports car to use the new 'corporate' front end style for the early-2000s.

- In 2003, MG showed off an experimental hybrid four-wheel-drive version of the TF, but insisted that it was only to be a one-off experiment.

It was the way in which this MG sports car could be up-graded 'in the showroom' – merely by studying the brochure and price lists before choosing some of the many options – which made it such an attractive car to the customers. As before, full air conditioning, a CD player, and a passenger-side safety airbag were all available, and on some models even the desirable anti-lock braking controls were extra, rather than standard.

All in all, the TF was an improvement over the MGF in almost every way, and not a single independent tester had any of those irritating 'why can't they …?' comments to make. The new car not only looked distinctly sharper – more trendy, even – than the old, but its handling was now much more sporty than that of the Hydragas-sprung MGF had ever been.

The changeover from the rather fluid ride offered by the Hydragas installation, to that offered by steel springs, was made very definitely, so that this latest car rode much stiffer than before, and felt altogether more sporting. With steering which felt to be much improved, this was an altogether uncompromising two-seater, one which even harked back a little to the original TF, and the MGA of the late 1950s which had replaced it. The change was so marked that one or two people even suggested that the new car was a little too hard – which made many other MG enthusiasts smile broadly.

The new car was so capable, though, that there were a few wistful requests for a 190bhp/KV6 derivative to be offered but MG-Rover insisted that this was one shoe-horn job which they could not consider.

Hood up or hood down, the TF of 2002 was a nicely-integrated shape.

SPECIFICATIONS

Production: Introduced in 2002

Body styles: Two-seater Roadster

Construction: Steel, unit-construction body/chassis

Engine: Four-cylinders, 1,589cc/1,796cc

Power Output: 114bhp to 158bhp

Transmission: Five-speed manual, six-speed manual, or optional automatic

Suspension: Front – independent, coil springs, rear – independent, coil springs

Brakes: Front discs, rear discs

Maximum speed: 118 mph (190 km/h) to 137 mph (220 km/h)

0-60mph (0-96 km/h): 9.2sec to 6.9 sec

(Below) The TF was a pure two seater, its fascia wrapped around the instruments and controls.

(Above) On the TF, the '160' denotes the power of the 1.8-liter K-Series engine.

(Below) Yet another style of light-alloy wheel for the TF of 2002.
(Right) Twin air bags, air conditioning, and electric window lifts – all part of the modern MG's equipment.

2003- *ZT 260*

Although MG's new management was badly restricted by a lack of working capital in the early 2000s, it took many brave decisions to keep the marque in the headlines. One of the bravest of all, undoubtedly, was to commission the ZT 260 V8, which was a real he-man's conversion of the ZT sedan.

By almost any commercial standards, this new model was bound to be an irrelevance, but MG was determined to produce a magnificent marque flagship, without having to spend a fortune on new press and assembly tooling. Although many rival engineers found the chosen technical solution difficult to understand, the result was a hairy-chested machine which would reach 155mph, which made it the fastest MG car of all time.

How was this done ? It is much easier to say this than to carry it out – but MG started from the bare bones of a front-wheel-drive ZT sedan, stripped out the complete running gear, engineered virtually a new underpan/platform, then installed a massive Ford Mustang V8 engine which drove the rear wheels. It was probably the most ambitious about-face, the most 'shoe-horn' job which had ever been tackled by a major British car maker -–yet from the outside of the car there was virtually no sign that this had been done.

Unless, that is, that one stood at the rear, saw the four exhaust outlets, and listened to the typically American wuffling noises which came out of them.

By 2003, although the base model, the Rover 75, had already been on sale for five years, the MG ZT derivative was still only two years old, the styling was extremely well-liked, and here was a car intended to give the entire marque that 'halo' effect which

the struggling MG-Rover group so desperately needed. If a limited-production model – and only up to 1,000 cars a year (just 20 cars every week) could be sold, it would do a great job.

When the first prototype was revealed in 2001 (actually to the media when the ZR/ZS/ZT types were being introduced), a car which was all sound, fury and vibrating panels, no-one took it seriously, and at that time it was no more than a 'good idea' rather than a serious project. It took two years to turn it into a very potent top-of-the-range model which, on performance terms at least, could compete with similarly-priced models from BMW, Jaguar and Mercedes-Benz.

The Ford V8 is a massive 4.6-liter unit, with single-overhead-camshaft cylinder heads and two valves per cylinder. This was somehow persuaded to fit into the ZT's engine bay in a 'north-south' attitude, there being very little clearance all round it to

Right: *The ZT 260 combined ZT body style with a Ford-USA engine and rear-wheel-drive.*

Below: *Except for its fat wheels and tires, the ZT 260 looked almost identical to the front-drive ZT models.*

the inner panels, and a major carve-up was needed to the floor pan to find space for the Tremec manual gearbox, the propeller shaft and the Dana Group rear axle, which contained a Hydratrak limited-slip differential.

Although the ZT-size tires and wheels were retained, the front suspension needed to be re-detailed Once again, space was a problem), and there was a completely different type of rear end, with five-link location of the rear wheels, all mounted into a sturdy new sub-frame. Bigger disc brakes front and rear all helped to keep the performance in check – this being necessary due to the Ford's 260bhp power output, and its massive 302lb.ft. of torque which was developed at 4,000rpm.

All this change would have been straightforward if MG had not also needed to make the new package comfortable, silent and refined, but it was all these aspects which took up so much time. The result was a car which looked very civilised, which had a very high level of equipment, and which could be driven either as a full-on sports sedan, or as one which could slip around town without any fuss. Surprisingly, MG did not make automatic transmission available – one was certainly available from Ford, who built Mustangs in this manner – but such a bulky transmission would have meant making an even bigger hump in the floor between the front passengers' legs.

Because this 260bhp machine was only meant to be produced in limited quantities, and was stuffed full of costly imported hardware, it was always going to be expensive, so there was no surprise when it was listed at £27,995 (before any extras were specified). As with other MGs, there were no plans to sell this model in North America, which meant that US enthusiasts would never learn just how different it could feel from the Mustang from which its power train was taken.

British drivers soon found that the 260 V8 felt, and behaved, completely differently from the basic ZT. Simply, when the gas pedal was pressed, here was a car which was thrust along by the rear wheels, rather than pulled by the fronts, and here was a car with a more favourable front/rear weight distribution ratio, and with power-assisted steering which did not also have to disguise the fact that the wheels it was turning were also driving the car.

Because the very high performance was matched to real refinement, and a supple ride, the 260 V8's character was more brutal, more overtly aggressive, and more purposeful than that of any previous MG. Although this was not naturally a high-revving engine, it was a real pleasure to urge the car along by regular gear-changes and know that there was always power, and torque, to spare.

If this car was a success, MG hinted, they would add even more powerful versions in the future, one of which would have a supercharged power unit. That, if it ever came to fruition., was bound to make MG drivers' eyes light up as never before.

(Left) On a car with so few flamboyant features, badging on the trunk lid was a good recognition point.

(Left) A V8 badge. Do you need any more hints?
(Below) ZT-T 260 – which, in MG-speak, means a wagon with 260bhp.

2003 ZT 260 V8

SPECIFICATIONS

Production: Introduced in 2003

Body styles: Four-door saloon/five-door estate

Construction: Steel, unit-construction, body/chassis

Engine: V8-cylinders, 4,601cc.

Power Output: 260bhp

Transmission: Five-speed manual

Suspension: Front – independent, coil springs, rear – independent, coil springs

Brakes: Front discs, rear discs

Maximum speed: 155 mph (250 km/h)

0-60mph (0-96 km/h): 6.2 sec

ZT-T 260

BU53 RXF

(Right) Normally found in US cars like the Ford Mustang, this massive 4.6-liter V8 engine filled the engine bay of the ZT 260.

2003- XPower SV

There was a great deal of history behind the birth of MG's new Xpower SV Supercar. The design was originally badged as a Qvale, and was to be built in Italy. The Qvale name reflected the company's owner, Qvale Automotive – and an earlier member of that US-based family had started in business by importing MG TCs into San Francisco in 1947.

MG-Rover's decision to buy the Qvale business was brave, but cost-effective, for the new Ford powered Mangusta, which had just gone haltingly on sale, came as part of the package. Unlike its rivals, the Mangusta's engine was up front, and drove the rear wheels – which was still the way that all purists liked their cars to be arranged. At that time Mangustas were steel-bodied and being built in Italy, but MG-Rover always intended to re-develop this car, and turn it into an MG.

The first concept car, or X80, was not liked when it was shown to the public in 2001, nor was the idea of making the cars in large numbers even economically feasible, so it was decided to move firmly up-market, up-performance, and to offer a car which could match, surpass even, the best of Ferrari and Maserati road cars. A decision to put such a much-modified version of this car into production came in March 2002. It was all set to be the fastest, the most extreme, and the most expensive MG road car of all time.

Below: *MG-Rover's Design Director, Peter Stevens, was mainly responsible for the style of the new XPower SV.*

It took far longer to get the new MG ready for sale than MG-Rover can ever have expected. Not only was the car changed from being a car with a retractable hardtop, to a fastback coupe, but it was given a completely new skin style which had been inspired by Design Director Peter Stevens. Then there were difficulties in working out how to continue having the galvanised steel chassis tubs made in Modena, the shells made nearby, then to get part-finished cars shipped over to Longbridge for final assembly – and of re-tuning the Ford-US running gear to make the car acceptable to UK and European customers.

MG finally previewed the re-designed 'X80' – or Xpower SV model - in October 2002, though the UK price of £75,000 for the 260bhp version was not set for another year, and the very first deliveries were delayed until the end of 2003. Along the way, most links with the original Qvale car, which had originated in the 1900s, were either abandoned, or much-changed.

The SV was an unashamed Supercar – one which was to be built with prestige and image in mind, rather than with a firm profit-making motive underpinning everything. Just 29 advance orders were placed for the car when it was displayed at the Birmingham Motor Show in October 2002, which helped MG to settled on a production rate of no more than three cars a week – maybe 120 – 130 cars a year – over a life cycle of four years.

The finalised SV was an Anglo-Italian hybrid which broke new ground for the way MG would do business. Mechanical assembly took place in a factory in Modena, using premises owned by Vaccari & Bosi, who produced the chassis tub itself. The body shell was constructed almost entirely from carbon-fibre, and was moulded by Opac in Turin. The Ford engine, and the five-speed gearbox (both generically like those used in the ZT 260 V8 sedan), were shipped in from Detroit. It was only after these had all been bolted together that the incomplete car was then transported to the UK for painting, trimming, testing, and onward delivery.

The style, by Peter Stevens, was radically different from that of the Qvale Mangusta which had provided the basics. Not only was it in carbon fibre, and not only was it a fastback coupe with a big. free-standing, rear spoiler, but it had its own unique line. The front grille echoed that of other Z-Series MGs, though in its own way, there were macho wheel arch flares, and big sills under the doors on each side of the shell itself.

Coming from a company which was still struggling to make a profit in 2003, in many ways this was a magnificently inappropriate

MILESTONE FACTS

- To get its hands on this new chassis, MG-Rover purchased the Qvale company of Italy

- In essence, the SV shared its engine and transmissions with the less-powerful MG ZT 260 V8

- The SV's chassis, body, and initial assembly were carried out in Italy. This was the first Italian-based MG of all time.

- The body shell of the SV was constructed out of weight-saving carbon fibre. This was the first time carbon had featured in an MG Road car.

- The SV's engine was a Ford V8, much-tuned. The same engine was also used in the Mustang.

- MG claimed that the most powerful version of the SV would reach 200mph – this easily making it the fastest MG road car of all time.

- The initial UK price of the SV was £75,000 that's $135000! – nearly three times that of the similarly-engined ZT 260 V8.

car. Sales would be extremely limited, the project could surely never be profitable, and unless it really could match the opposition from other Supercar makers it might soon die for lack of sales. MG-Rover knew all this, but took the Brave Pill, gritted their teeth, and set the SV to do its job.

The style, the rumbling character, the tire – stripping performance (particularly in the optional higher powered forms), and the sports-racing type of ride and handling, all meant that this was going to be a car for the few. In every way this was an elitist MG, and director Stevens had insisted on an aggressive shape which emphasised all those things. It was not a quiet car, and not even a particularly civilised car – nor ever meant to be so – but it certainly delivered on the promise of its super-high performance.

There were those who thought that the SV had no more relevance to MG's modern business that Ford's GT40 had been to Ford in the 1960s – but you only have to see what the earlier car had done to boost the company's image to see why it excited so many top men at Longbridge. And, as Stevens once admitted:

'It's a bit cruise-missile-like, a dangerous weapon that we reckon is as exciting to drive as it looks.'

Only time, and enough MG enthusiasts with a well-stocked wallet, would prove him right.

(Left) The SV';s rear end was all function – with a spoiler to provide downforce, and twin exhaust outlets.

(Right) Five spoke wheels and ultra-low profile tires were all part of the SV's Supercar image.

(Above) Air outlets behind the front wheelarches, necessary to get hot air out of the engine bay.

(Right) Racing-type seats and full harness belts. No compromises in the SV interior.

SPECIFICATIONS

Production: Introduced in 2003

Body styles: Two-seater fixed-head coupe

Construction: Steel chassis tub, carbon-fibre body

Engine: V8-cylinders, 4,601cc.

Power Output: 260bhp/402bhp

Transmission: Five-speed manual

Suspension: Front – independent, coil springs, rear – independent, coil springs

Brakes: Front disc, rear discs

Maximum speed: 165mph (265kph)/200mph (322 km/h)

0-60mph (0-96 km/h): 5.3sec/4.4secs

1922 | **1923** | **1924** | **1925** | **1926** | **1927** | **1928** | **1929** | **1930** | **1931** | **1932** | **1933**

1922 Cecil Kimber joined Morris garages as General Manager

Above: Abingdon production in 1930.

1923 Kimber inspired the first Morris Garages 'Chummy Models'.
• First ever MGs, the Raworth-bodied cars, produced.

1924 Launch of original MG-badged cars, the 14/28 Super Sports.
• Assembly centred at Albert Lane, Oxford.

1925 MG assembly moved to Bainton Road, Oxford.

1927 MG assembly moved to a new factory at Edmund Road, Cowley, Oxford

Left: the 1927 14/40

1928 Introduction of the very first Midget, the 847cc M-Type.

1929 MG business relocated to Abingdon, where it would remain until 1980

Above: Proud radiator and octagon badge, the F-Type Magna was so typical of 1930s MG styling.

1946 | **1947** | **1948** | **1949** | **1950** | **1951** | **1952** | **1953** | **1954** | **1955** | **1956** | **1957**

(Above) YA assembly at Abingdon, in the late 1940s

1947 Introduction of the Y-Type saloon, the first MG with independent front suspension

1950 Introduction of the TD Midget, the first Midget with independent front suspension

Below: the 1951 YA Sedan

Above: bagge from the 1954 ZA Magnette

1954 Design/engineering returned to Abingdon, preparatory to introducing the MGA

1952 Nuffield – and MG - became part of the British Motor Corporation (BMC).

1953 Introduction of the ZA Magnette – the first BMC-inspired saloon

1955 Last T-Series Midgets built. MGA prototypes raced at Le Mans. Launch of new-styleMGA.

1934 **1935** **1936** **1937** **1938** **1939** **1940** **1941** **1942** **1943** **1944** **1945**

Above: the 1936 TA Midget

1935 Lord Nuffield sold the MG Car Co. to his Nuffield Organisation. The motorsport programme was killed off. Design/engineering moved to Cowley, Oxford.
• Introduction of the first 'Cowley' MG, the SA 2-liter

1936 Introduction of TA Midget, the first ohv-engined Midget.
• Introduction of VA 1.5-liter model

1939 World War Two began. MG car assembly ended late in the year.

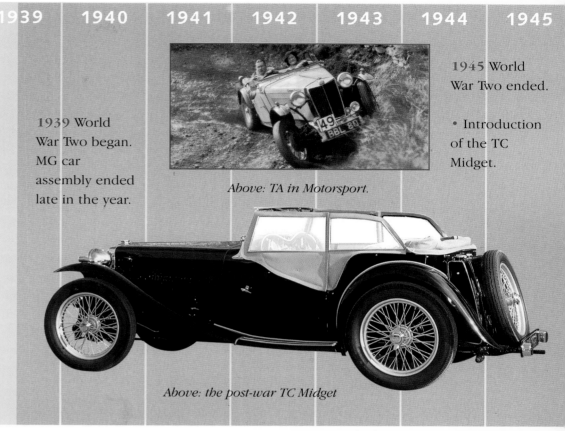

Above: TA in Motorsport.

1945 World War Two ended.

• Introduction of the TC Midget.

Above: the post-war TC Midget

1958 **1959** **1960** **1961** **1962** **1963** **1964** **1965** **1966** **1967** **1968** **1969**

1958 Introduction of MGA Twin-Cam, the first twin-cam engined MG road car.
• Introduction of the Austin-Healey Sprite, built at Abingdon, and forerunner of new-generation Midget

1961 Launch of new-generation Midget, based on Austin-Healey Sprite design

1962 Last MGA (1600 Mk II) built – this being the last-ever separate-chassis MG [Unless you count the X power SV]

1968 BMC became part of the new British Leyland Motor Corporation

Left: The Midget was a best-seller from 1961.

1963 Introduction of MGB, which the best-selling MG of all time.
• Introduction of MG1100 saloon, the first transverse-engined front-wheel-drive MG

1967 Introduction of MGC, a six-cylinder derivative of the MGB

Above: a 1961 MGA ex Works Coupe

1959 MG Magnette Mk III went into production, but at Cowley

Right: the 1967 MGC Roadster

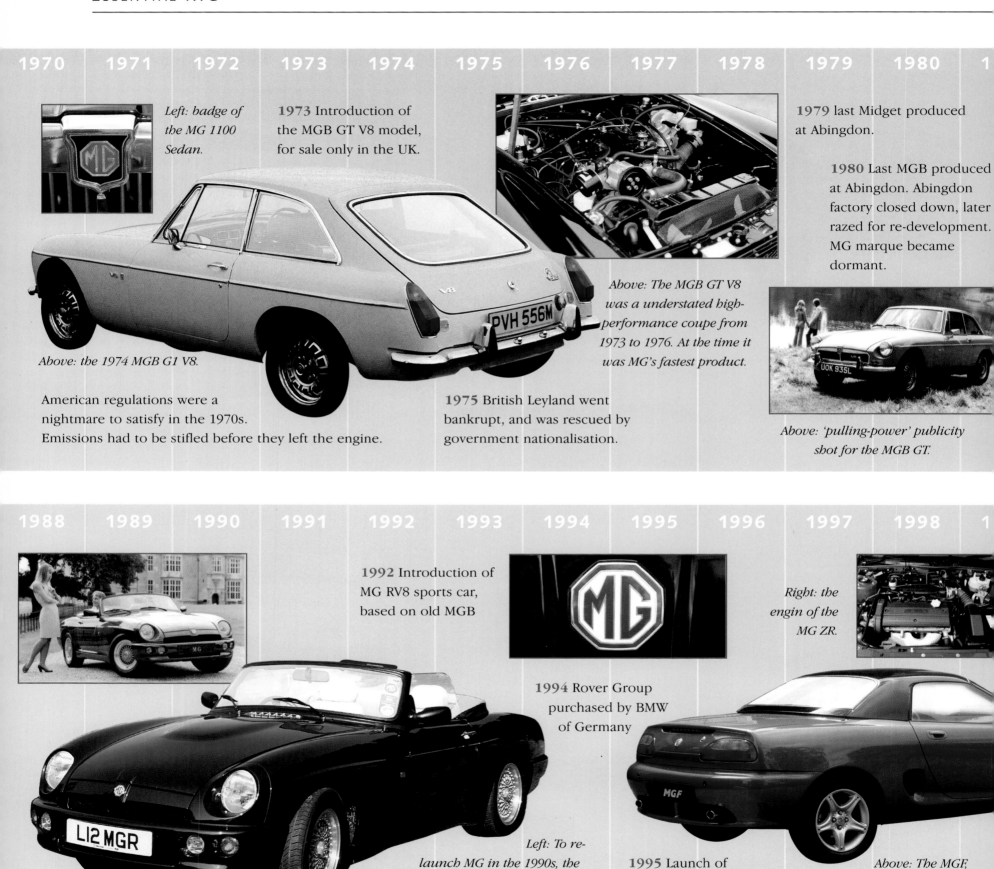

1970 **1971** **1972** **1973** **1974** **1975** **1976** **1977** **1978** **1979** **1980** 1

Left: badge of the MG 1100 Sedan.

1973 Introduction of the MGB GT V8 model, for sale only in the UK.

1979 last Midget produced at Abingdon.

1980 Last MGB produced at Abingdon. Abingdon factory closed down, later razed for re-development. MG marque became dormant.

Above: The MGB GT V8 was a understated high-performance coupe from 1973 to 1976. At the time it was MG's fastest product.

Above: the 1974 MGB G1 V8.

American regulations were a nightmare to satisfy in the 1970s. Emissions had to be stifled before they left the engine.

1975 British Leyland went bankrupt, and was rescued by government nationalisation.

Above: 'pulling-power' publicity shot for the MGB GT.

1988 **1989** **1990** **1991** **1992** **1993** **1994** **1995** **1996** **1997** **1998** 1

1992 Introduction of MG RV8 sports car, based on old MGB

1994 Rover Group purchased by BMW of Germany

Right: the engin of the MG ZR.

Left: To re-launch MG in the 1990s, the company offered the RV8, Only 2,000 were built: many were sold in Japan.

1995 Launch of new mid-engined MGF sports car

Above: The MGF, introduced in 1995, was the first-ever mid-engined MG sports car.

1982 1983 1984 1985 1986 1987

1982 MG revived, on Metro and Metro Turbo models. Henceforth, all MGs would be built at Longbridge, Birmingham (home of Austin-Rover, later of Rover Group).

Below: the 1986 MG Metro Turbo

1985 production of 200 MG Metro 6R4s – mid-engined four-wheel-drive rally cars

1984 Introduction of Austin-based MG Montego sedan

1983 Introduction of Austin-based MG Maestro hatchback

Left: the dashboard of a MG Metro Turbo

2000 2001 2003 2004 2005 2006

2000 BMW sold off Rover to new management team. New concern re-named itself MG-Rover.

2001 Introduction of Rover-based ZR (hatchback), ZS (sedan) and ZT (sedan) models, based on Rover 25, 45 and 75 ranges

Above: the 2003 XPower SV

2003 Introduction of ZT 260V*, a front-engine/rear-drive conversion of the ZT, with Ford-V8 engine.
• Introduction of Xpower SV Supercar MG, based on re-developed Qvale sports car design.

PRODUCTION FIGURES

14/28 and 14.40	c.1,300
18/80 Six	741
M-Type Midget	3,235
F-Type Magna	1,250
J1/J2 Midget	2,463
K3 Magnette	33
L-Type Magna	576
PA/PB Midget	2,526
N-Type and KN Magnette	946
SA '2-Liter'	2,738
TA and TB Midget	3,382
VA '1½-Liter'	2,407
WA '2.6-liter'	369
TC	10,000
Y-Type '1¼-liter'	7,459
YT Tourer	877
TD Midget	29,664
ZA/ZB Magnette	36,600
TF Midget	9,600
MGA 1600	31,501
MGA Twin-Cam	2,111
Magnette Mk III/Mk IV	29,414
Midget	224,839
MGB Mk 1	137,733
MG 1100 and 1300	143,067
MGC	8,999
MGB Mk II	375,147
MGB GT V8	2,591
Metro and Metro Turbo	142,175
RV8	2,000
MGF	77,269
ZR	Current model
ZT	Current model
MG TF	Current model
ZT 260 V8	Current model
Xpower SV	Current model

Index

Acknowledgments

Special thanks to the MG Owners Club in particular Richard Monk .
Thanks for the tour of the workshop.
MG-Rover Marketing Dept: special thanks to Kevin Jones and Helen.
Andrew Morland for his help in the early stages.
Graham Robson: if only all authors were like him!
Phil Clucas for stunning layouts.

Picture Credits

All Color pictures up to P133-MG Owners Club- copyright Richard Monk.
Images from P133-155 courtesy of MG-Rover.
All monochrome- Graham Robson.